From her humble ice cream shed in London, ice cream
obsessive Kitty Travers has reimagined the way we see our
favorite flavors, focusing on peak-season produce combined
with unexpected herbs, spices, and mix-ins. Her frozen
combinations are deliciously eye-opening: Pineapple and
Lemongrass; Nectarine and Tarragon; Sea Salt, Rosemary &
Pine Nut; and Chocolate Treacle, to name a few. The creative
recipes in *La Grotta* will inspire home cooks to explore
making ice cream and ices in deliciously bold, new ways.

# LA GROTTA

**Kitty Travers**

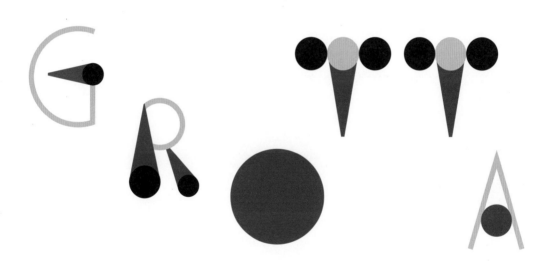

**Ice Creams and Sorbets**

Clarkson Potter/Publishers

New York

# Contents

Note—Features pages are
listed in italics.

# INTRODUCTION

Ice cream was not so hot when I was growing up. It was usually limited to the summertime treat of a 9 pence orange Sparkle (a fluorescent ice pop) in the park after school, or the occasional slice of a supermarket's economy sticky yellow vanilla brick (a rectangular length of ice cream wrapped in cardboard). This would melt and refreeze over the course of being served from its damp box, and turn into a curious foamy gum. But I still loved it.

As a teenager living at home in suburban Twickenham my favorite cookbook was *Cuisine of the Sun* by Roger Vergé, an inheritance from my godmother (and one half of the Two Fat Ladies), Jennifer Patterson. The recipes in it demonstrate the use of simple harmonies to enhance the flavor of each ingredient, while still allowing the beautiful, natural produce of Provence to shine. Vergé called it "cuisine heureuse." It left me pining for something brighter than the supermarket foods I'd grown up with . . . something transportive and sun-kissed.

It was a relief to leave school, which I hated and had only a string of failed A levels to show for. I went to art school and, to pay the bills, got a job at age 18 working as a greengrocer on the forecourt of the Bluebird Garage on the King's Road. I spent a lot of time spraying arugula with an atomizer, while the real work was done by Alf. He arrived early from the market in Milan with a van full of beautiful fruits and vegetables, from moonlight-yellow pears wrapped in inky, indigo sugar paper to bunches of dusky black grapes tied with shiny lilac florist ribbon.

I dropped out of art school and spent the summer of 2000 in Marseille instead. On my return to London I read a newspaper article about a man called Lionel Poilâne who was opening a bakery in London to make this stuff called sourdough bread. I got the bus straight over to the Pimlico shop to find the doors wide open and the shop still being built, with Monsieur Poilâne overseeing the installation of a vast brick oven. I was emboldened after my summer speaking French and introduced myself to him, winning myself the position of Poilâne's first (and—for some years—only) British shop girl.

## Paris

It was a hard sell at the beginning, with the bread at an eye-watering £5.90 per loaf. People would come in asking if we made sandwiches or sausage rolls or pies, and we had to try and encourage them to taste the bread: the miraculous flavor of its crackling crust a result of the magic that can be achieved from just a few essential ingredients: flour, water, and salt. I worked as an assistant at the London shop and spent some time at the Paris branch. In Paris I lived in a room above the bakery itself, and the smell of those huge burnished loaves of sourdough bread baking in the ancient brick ovens got me out of bed to work at 5:30 every morning. But although I loved that company, and the chewy crust of that bread, I was looking for something else.

Each morning during the spring of 2001 as I got ready for work I had the telly on in the background. It was screening live segments from the Cannes Film Festival. A clip showed pop stars singing on the beach and their hair looked really shiny. It seemed glamorous and appealing. Then I remembered that Roger Vergé, author of my favorite cookbook, had a restaurant and cooking school in Cannes.

Poilâne was friends with Vergé and when I handed in my notice and bought a one-way ticket to Nice, he handed me a personal letter of recommendation to give to him. He asked Vergé to take care of me and wrote that I sold bread "as though I were selling diamonds." I still have that letter in a suitcase, because pathetically I was too shy to give it to Mr. Vergé. I didn't have the confidence to work in a real kitchen. But I couldn't face going home, and so instead I took a waitressing job at a beachfront hotel, and started a new career as Cannes' worst waitress.

## Cannes

It was incredibly unglamorous. I worked 16-hour shifts in tennis shoes, nude tights, and a pleated aertex miniskirt. But that was when I found an ice cream shop—a little *glacière* with tinted glass windows and green leather banquettes just off the Croissette—and began a daily ritual. After a swim in the sea and before work, I would eat ice cream sundaes for breakfast.

The menu board changed daily and the flavors dazzled me: *cerise, abricot, cassis, groseille, saffran,* and *calisson*. It was nothing like ice cream in the UK. I was astonished by the texture and how they captured the fresh taste of an ingredient in a frozen scoop. I puzzled over how it was made, and the ice cream seed was planted.

On my days off I took the train along the coast to Italy. Ice cream specialities in Piedmonte were hazelnut, coffee, and latte Alpina—even violet *Pinguino's* (choc ices)—and in Liguria, green lemon and bergamot. People seemed to go for an ice cream and a walk the way we in the UK go to the pub. I walked and walked, discovering markets and eating ice creams.

Back home that winter, working another stopgap deli job, I read *The Man Who Ate Everything* by Jeffrey Steingarten. My favorite chapter was "The Mother of All Ice Cream," about his search for the best gelato in the world. I had a plan. Summoning the help of all the Italians working in my deli, I wrote letters to every place mentioned in the book. I attached my CV and asked to be given a chance to apprentice and learn the art of making ice cream. I posted the applications and waited patiently. I didn't get a single reply.

## New York

There was nowhere in the UK in which you could learn ice cream making back then. But in 2002, I inherited a generous sum of money from my grandmother. After sitting on it for some time, I decided to enroll in a proper chef diploma course ... in New York. I feebly hoped that afterward I might be able to get work experience for Jeffrey Steingarten.

What I didn't expect was what happened at culinary school; I loved every second of it, and for the first time in my life I started doing well at something. My head teacher— Chef Ted—said he'd pay thirty bucks at Daniel's to eat my coconut ice cream. I still remember the feeling of my skin stinging as it flushed pink with happiness.

The creativity and energy of what I experienced food-wise in New York wasn't tied to the old European traditions we still hang on to in Britain. There was such positivity and invention! I snipped an article out of the *New York Times* listing the city's best ice creams, from pumpkin at Ciao Bella to lychee and red bean at the Chinatown Ice Cream Factory; when my course finished I went to "stage" (work for free) at my favorite of them all: Otto Enoteca, a pizza and gelato joint that was already famous for its olive oil gelato with sea salt and strawberries. This was really something. The head pastry chef at Otto was a curly-haired, bandanna-wearing, old school New Yorker called Meredith Kurtzman. She had a sensitivity for putting flavors together that was original but never sensationalist, and was

scrupulous about the pure taste of the ingredients shining through. I was happiest when I was sent to Union Square Greenmarket on Monday and Wednesday mornings to buy ingredients. My heart was bursting with pride to be walking the streets of New York in my clean chef's whites, and to feel part of that city. It was late autumn and I would come back to the restaurant with crates of pecan nuts, pumpkin, fresh corn, and Concord grapes and tins of Grade 3 maple syrup, all to be spun into delicious ice creams.

New York was still swelteringly hot, and at the end of the day I'd fill a container with house-made granita in tart berry flavors. The bar would top it up with soda water and a straw, and, sipping it slowly, I'd make my way home to the tiny East Village studio I shared with a small mouse and a quite large cockroach.

I would have stayed if I could, but my visa was about to end. So I spent my remaining few free days doing stages. One was at Prune. Gabrielle Hamilton was another dazzler. She approved of my apartment having no air-con, and told me not to be afraid of the heat when I was given the task of grilling bream one service; instead, she said I should get closer to the fiery flames. Most important, she told me a new kind of restaurant had opened in London: St. John Bread & Wine. She said I should go back and get a job with Fergus Henderson.

## London

It was 11 a.m. and the tables in the dining room at St. John had been pulled together and laid for staff lunch. In the open kitchen trays of fat, pink freshly boiled Scottish langoustines lay steaming by open windows while Justin the baker was setting warm caraway seed and buttery eccles cakes out on the counter.

I was allowed to stage that day, and at the end of it was offered the job of pastry chef. In all I spent five years working for Fergus at St. John Bread & Wine and then for his wife, Margot, at the Rochelle Canteen. It was the greatest happiness I had known up to that point. All us chefs were utterly devoted to Fergus and Justin and worked incredibly hard for them. But what was special about St. John was its humanity. It wasn't assumed that you had to suffer to create beautiful food. Or contort the ingredients. Dishes were presented simply to highlight the beauty of the ingredient (they were mostly British) and not the ego of the chef. It was unprecedented and brave at a time when most cooking in the UK was looking outward for inspiration. A revelation for me was receiving a tray of Kentish strawberries one day in the first week of June. Small and fragrant and rosy red all the way through like sweeties, they seemed miraculous.

The very first ice cream I made at St. John was fresh mint. I peeped across the kitchen to the dining room, and watched with delight as the lady who had ordered it paused, looked down at her bowl with surprise, and smiled.

Meanwhile, every holiday I had I went to Italy, making my way to each gelateria mentioned in Jeffrey Steingarten's old essay—on returning to St. John I was able to test out new recipes from what I'd learned.

## Sicily, Rome, Naples

Backpacking with my sister in Sicily one summer, I ended up eating tangerine sorbet in Caffé Sicilia in Noto, and asking the waiter questions about how it was made. He told me that years before, they had had a funny letter from an English girl asking about their ice creams. I was taken into the kitchen and there was my old letter pinned to the wall, complete with passport photo. The elderly owner of the café came out to talk to me. He showed me around the kitchen, giving me a piece of marzipan to taste made from almonds from neighboring Avola and a lumpy lemon. He communicated that although he was sympathetic, I could never learn how to make ice cream like an Italian—we couldn't have the same understanding of ingredients, because he had been making it since he was *"cosi!"*... and gestured to knee height.

Well, there's nothing like being told you can't do something to spur you on. I decided then and there that I wanted to make ice cream with the same skill and understanding that this man had. But, instead of trying to copy what Italians do so well already, I would try to do my own thing—something relevant to the place I came from—and make it perfect.

I left St. John to set up La Grotta Ices and spent a few months cheffing for Margot Henderson and Melanie Arnold while I saved up to buy my ice cream van. One morning while I was chopping beets (wrongly, as Margot pointed out, "Argh... No! You gotta still be able to see the SHAPE of the beet!"), Margot mentioned that the night before she had been sitting next to Alice Waters (the pioneering chef-restaurateur and force behind the sustainable food movement in California) at a fund-raising dinner. Alice had recently founded a kitchen at the American Academy in Rome where they hoped to feed the community of the academy using locally grown, seasonal organic produce. They needed volunteers. I sent a postcard to Alice at her restaurant Chez Panisse and waited. Six months later, I was on a night train to Rome, where I lived and worked for a winter, before returning to making ices again in the spring.

Working abroad during the off season became an annual habit. The winter after that I moved to Naples. I pictured myself renting a charming room in a crumbling villa and topping up my winter tan on a balcony cascading with lemons. I'd find a job, shop in the market every day, eat ice cream, and maybe I'd try to write, too.

What I discovered when I got there (apart from the fact that it was freezing cold and rained almost every day for three months) was that this situation doesn't really exist in Naples. There are no flats to rent for single professionals. Single people live at home with their families until they get married... and then they stay living at home some more. Instead, I took a long-term lease on a room in a B&B. Living with a depressed (he ate a LOT of Nutella) 19-year-old boy and his pet chinchilla was not what I'd had in mind, but never mind—I pounded the streets of Naples for hours each day, eating *pizza fritta* and *sfogliatelle,* and tried to look for work.

In Naples I worked at two restaurants. A chef friend in London had tipped me off about somewhere he'd had a good meal, so I went there first. The two women running the kitchen looked at me with deep suspicion and asked what the hell I thought I was doing. Didn't I know there was a crisis in Italy? There wasn't enough work for Italians, let alone foreigners. Plus I towered over both of them and was too big for the kitchen. Nevertheless, I could come a few evenings a week and do work experience if I wanted to learn. It was pretty terrifying. Rita and Nuncia used to fight with each other like wildcats—occasionally breaking off to complain that I was rolling the rice balls too slowly—and would then attack one another again and have to be dragged apart by the always-amused head waiter. Sometimes I'd catch Rita looking me slowly up and down . . . *"L'altezza è mezza bellezza"* (half of beauty is height), she would mutter bitterly before turning away with a sigh.

I managed to get another day job, but the only place that would take me was a trendy modern restaurant where the owner was a bit of a celebrity and the food sucked—the pasta was gluey, and the fish was vacuum packed and sous-vided to obliteration.

Nevertheless, Naples was good. Piaggio Ape's served as impromptu market stalls all over town, piled high with artichokes that I gorged on—3 euros for a bunch of ten. Coffee everywhere was dementedly good and thick, as only the first oil-rich drips made it into your drink—the scalding hot cup was whisked away leaving the rest of the coffee to pour away into the drain. I would picture the underground pipes of Naples flowing with espresso.

## La Grotta Ices

Now I am the happy owner of La Grotta Ices, finally established in 2008. The name comes from the Italian for "cave" or "grotto," and it was named as such in homage to the first cool, dark ice cream shop that I discovered working in Cannes, and which set me off on my journey.

At first the ice creams were made at home, with two freezers in a bedroom, then under a damp brick railway arch in Bermondsey. Since 2009, they have been created in my workshop or "ice cream shed," a converted Victorian greengrocer in a beautiful historical south London square.

The La Grotta Ices range changes weekly. My intent is to create inventive, not-too-sweet ice creams that capture the bright flavor of exquisite, ripe fruit but with a supernaturally light, smooth, and sublime texture. The focus is on using minimally processed, fresh, whole ingredients and using the confines of the seasons and simple methods to do so. Ices are sold from the back of a small white Piaggio Ape—the same vehicle used to sell fruits and vegetables in Neapolitan markets.

La Grotta runs from April to December. I sell scoops at markets and art fairs, and tubs in shops around London, and in between that teach a long-established class in ice cream making at the award-winning School of Artisan Foods in Nottinghamshire. For the first three months of the year—when it's too cold to sell ice cream (it doesn't melt in the mouth properly at temperatures below 57°F)—I continue to work abroad.

## What's the Difference Between Ice Cream and Gelato?

It is a question that tormented me for many years. And that many people ask me. The literal answer is that gelato is just the Italian word for ice cream . . . but here's what most people will also explain:

1. Gelato is made with mostly milk and rarely contains egg yolks (ice cream is generally custard-based). Gelato is consequently lower in fat.

2. Gelato is churned more slowly than ice cream, which means it incorporates less air into the mix and is a denser, smoother product compared to ice cream. Less air means that the flavor of the gelato is more concentrated.

3. Gelato is served at a higher temperature than ice cream so that it has a soft texture and can be scooped easily.

What you will never hear anyone (particularly gelato makers) explain is just how they create all of these wonderful attributes. It's as though it happened by magic!

In most cases, gelato compensates for the lower fat and less air by adding commercially used ingredients less familiar to the home cook. Dry milk powder (milk solids) adds richness and body to the gelato, making the texture seem creamier and more dense. This is because although it is fat-free, it is high in milk proteins. Sugars like glucose, dextrose, and trimoline allow the gelato to stay soft and scoopable as though freshly churned, but because they don't have the sweetness of saccharose (sugar), the gelato doesn't taste as sweet. They also help prevent crystallization, which keeps the gelato smooth.

I choose not to use either in my ice creams for a few reasons. First, dry milk powder has a "cooked" taste that interrupts the sweet, pure flavor of fresh cream and milk. Likewise, glucose, dextrose, and trimoline tend to coat your tongue. Sugar is much "cleaner" tasting and allows the other flavors to shine. But there are other issues to consider apart from taste. Dry milk powder contains roughly 50 percent lactose compared with fresh whole milk, which is 4.8 percent. Skimmed milk powder is a prevalent ingredient in many processed foods, and as people are consuming lactose in much higher quantities than we used to, it wouldn't be surprising to me if this turned out to be one of the causes of lactose intolerance.

### The perfect balance

You don't have to use mysterious powders to make great ice cream. The foundations of a perfect scoop are based on having the right quantity of water, sugar, fat, solids (proteins), and emulsifier in a recipe, all of which are found in milk, cream, and fresh eggs. Whole fruits add body. These ingredients need to be frozen quickly while being stirred/churned. This incorporates some air (to keep the ice cream light) and ensures the ice crystals are as small and even as possible (to keep the ice cream smooth).

Ice cream recipes have to be perfectly balanced to work. If you remove one element—like the fat—for example, your ice cream will suffer and lose "body," becoming thin and watery. Likewise, if you take away the sugar, your recipe will freeze into a hard icy block and be impossible to scoop. A well-balanced recipe will stand you in good stead.

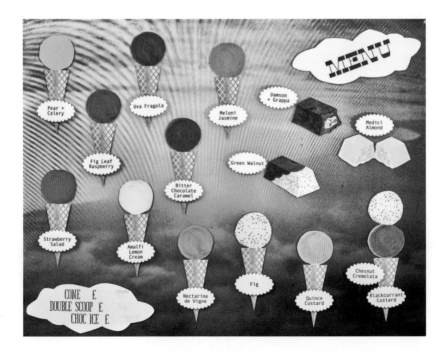

# How to Use This Book

●—●

I now have 13 years' worth of crispy-edged, custard-splattered recipe notebooks (and counting) in which I've recorded all my ice cream making attempts. The early books are experimental—recipes I tried once or twice and didn't go back to. Throughout the middle ones you start to recognize the favorites that I return to, making small changes and adjustments with each more recent version. This book contains all the recipes that made it into the most recent notebook—the core favorites. They have been honed and edited to leave only those that work and are delicious, ones that I look forward to returning to year after year.

The order in which the recipes have been printed follows the spectrum of ices make throughout the year. The "menu" is constantly changing as ingredients come in and go out of season. You can dip in and out of the book as you like, but if you use it as a seasonal guide you will find fruits that are more likely to be ripe, which means they taste good and are at their best value.

The book begins in January, mid-winter, a dry time for locally grown produce and a time when I welcome piercingly bright citrus fruits into my kitchen. Amalfi lemons, leafy navel oranges, and bergamot from Italy come into season now, followed by sweet and sour kumquats and the extraordinary blood orange with its pitted peel heavy with rich oils and its volcanic strawberry-flavored tangy flesh—it's exciting!

In February, I give in to the lure of dazzling tropical fruits from overseas. The vivid colors and potent flavors of pineapple, passion fruit, papaya, lime, and mango bring energy to this somewhat bleak time of year.

Early spring ice creams employ the use of bracing kiwi, earthy rhubarb, confetti-like rice, peach leaves, and delicate scented blossoms like mimosa and clover. In late May, expect the first cherries from the South of France and the Gariguette strawberry from Brittany. British strawberries should be ripe and red all the way through by June and are swiftly followed by soft-skinned stone fruits: flat white peaches, apricots, and nectarines.

By mid-summer my ice cream scooping freezer displays a gorgeous selection of pinks, reds, and purples: custards and water ices stained from juicy berries, blackcurrants, and pêche de vigne.

Autumn is a rich time for grapes, figs, melons, and plums. Then later on, apple, pear, and quince make fragrant ice creams—perfect for serving alongside a slice of fruit pie as the temperature drops and the air becomes fresher. Fresh fruits are less available come November and so I turn to richer flavorings to use in ice creams—chestnuts, almonds, pine nuts, pistachio, malt, dried fruits, and warm butterscotch. To celebrate the year coming to a close the recipes become more festive—ricotta with candied fruit peel, Barbadian rum custard, and also clementine and spiced lime sorbets.

My recipes are less sweet and have a slightly lower fat content compared to "super premium" ice cream. The reason for this is that I like the flavors to be bright and not too inhibited by heavy cream and sugar. In my opinion, they are the perfect balance of fresh fruit, milk, cream, and sugar—rich and satisfying, with a good body and "mouthfeel." This does mean, though, that it's a good idea to place the ice cream in the fridge for 10 minutes before serving, to make it more scoopable. If you prefer a richer-tasting ice cream, you can swap the amount of milk for half-and-half in each recipe to no detriment.

# Ingredients

One thing about not using the more commercially used ice cream ingredients at La Grotta Ices (such as dry milk powder/glucose/dextrose) is that the home cook can make exactly the same recipes that I make. Recipes have been scaled down to domestic size and can be replicated at home with the same success. Teaching my regular ice cream making classes at the School of Artisan Food over the past seven years gives me a chance to test them out!

If you feel the same way about minimally processed ingredients, you can start by choosing good dairy, like organic heavy cream and milk from trustworthy sources that support the dairy industry. Buy good eggs, free-range at least, please, because factory farming is gross. Large ones work best for these recipes. I like using Turbinado sugar (you only need superfine sugar for cake-making, though you can use it if you prefer) as it lends a delicious rounded depth to the ice cream and is unrefined. Unless otherwise stated, all the recipes in this book use unrefined granulated.

In an ideal world you might use fruit you've either grown or picked yourself. Failing that, I recommend shopping at farmers' markets or ethnic markets (where the produce is often cheap and ripe), or buying from independent shops who care about sourcing the good stuff. Picking your own from fruit farms gives you an opportunity to find harder-to-source ingredients like blackcurrant and peach leaves. Ask first but it's really unlikely anybody would miss a few leaves. Give fruit a good sniff before buying it and choose that with the best perfume. Fruits will always taste best and be sweetest when they're in season and this is important when using them for ice cream, as you want the flavor to be strong and bright.

Some ingredients might be difficult to come by—like mulberries. But the point isn't that this is something you can have whenever you want . . . it's a treat to make perhaps just once a year when you find that special cache—and remember it for the rest of the year.

If a recipe doesn't require using an entire fruit (say you've bought a really big pineapple) then use the part from the flower end first. Most fruits (except berries, which are uniformly sweet) have a flower end where the blossom used to grow, and a stem end where the fruit attached to a branch. The flower end is always the sweetest part and will make your ice cream or sorbet taste as good as it can. Test this out the next time you eat an apple!

Unless you live in a place where you get gluts of ripe fruit, good ingredients are expensive, so be economical wherever possible to maximize their use. Unwaxed citrus peels can be used for candying; lemon and clementine leaves can be steeped in sugar syrup and used to add an extra dimension to sorbet and granita. After sieving berries you can use the seeds to make "pip juice." Just mix them in a jug with cold water and chill in the fridge overnight before straining the next day and—ta-daa!—a gem-colored free fruit squash! Likewise, if you are able to pick your own fruits, infusing ice cream bases with peach, fig, or blackcurrant leaves or fresh herbs makes a simple ice into something unique and extraordinary and impossible to replicate in a shop-bought product. Ice cream is a great carrier of flavor, so have fun experimenting—just Google to check whether it's safe to eat first! (I once had to pour gallons of precious lily-of-the-valley-flavored ice cream down the drain after I discovered I'd infused the custard with poison.)

Vanilla pods also are such an extraordinary ingredient—derived from an orchid—and expensive, too. It's crazy not to get the most use out of them possible.

Split pods lengthwise to scrape the seeds out, then add both pod and seeds to the milk as it's heating. Once the custard is aged, scoop out the pod, rinse in cold water, and leave to dry for a day. The pods can then be kept in a sugar jar for a few weeks to flavor your baking sugar. I hear you yawning . . . but at this point, you can advance vanilla thriftiness to another level: remove the brittle sugary pods and poke them into a three-quarters-full bottle of cheap vodka—the cheapest you like. Every time you use a vanilla pod, add it to the bottle until you can't squeeze any more in. At this point, write the date on the bottle and hide it somewhere for six months. When you look at it again it will have become a half-gallon of viscous black vanilla extract. Not for vodka shots, but perfect for any recipe that calls for vanilla extract and at a fraction of the cost of the shop-bought stuff.

## Methods

Wash fruits (unless specified not to) in a sink full of clean, cold water then place on clean dish towels to dry.

In ice cream recipes where the fruits are to be used fresh and raw, I almost always recommend macerating them in a mixture of sugar and lemon juice. This draws color and flavor from their skins and intensifies their flavor. Cooked fruit also intensifies in color after some resting time in the fridge. Both parts of the recipe, the fruit and custard, should be the same cold temperature when they are mixed together before churning. This helps to preserve the bright color of the ice cream and avoids the possibility of the custard splitting, which can easily happen otherwise because of the fruit's natural acidity.

When making sugar syrups, there is no need to weigh out your sugar and water separately. Remember that cups and ounces are interchangeable when it comes to water—so just weigh your sugar, then add the water to the same bowl or pan until it reaches the desired weight.

Tempering refers to mixing the uncooked egg yolks and sugar together, before slowly adding the hot milk and cream in a way that avoids scrambling the eggs. To do this, mix the yolks and sugar together with a whisk, and then pour most of the hot dairy liquid over them in a slow stream, whisking constantly. Leave a little milk at the bottom of the pan each time to prevent the base of the pan from scorching. Whisk well to dissolve the sugar and any lumps of yolk, then pour the mix back into the same pan and cook out over low heat to 82°C/180°F, stirring constantly to make the custard.

Take care not to mix the sugar and yolks together too early on; only do this once the milk and cream are hot and steamy. Sugar (and salt) both have the effect of setting the proteins in the egg yolks and will make hard yellow lumps in your custard if they sit together for too long first.

The ice cream base (or custard) should be cooked to 82°C/180°F in every recipe where dairy or egg yolks are used. This is called pasteurization and the reasons behind it are twofold: first, the custard base only thickens at 80°C/176°F (this is the stage when most recipe books refer to the custard as being able to "coat the back of a spoon") and this makes your base much silkier and richer in texture compared to an uncooked one. Second, it ensures that if there happen to be harmful bacteria in the dairy or eggs—unlikely nowadays, but still possible—they will be killed off at this temperature. There's no point trying to guess this stage when digital thermometers are inexpensive and provide a quick, efficient way of monitoring the temperature. The custard should be stirred constantly as it heats up, otherwise the mixture may scorch or overcook in the corners of the pan, scrambling the eggs. Use a heatproof silicone spatula to do this so that it gets into the corners, or a heart-spring whisk rather than an old wooden spoon (which have a tendency to smell like bolognese sauce—at least mine do). Keep a close eye on the pan and never let the mix boil, as this will also split the custard.

Use a heavy-based, non-reactive pan made from stainless steel to cook your custards, and for when you cook fruit. Other metals like aluminium may react to the acids in the fruit, causing discoloration and a "tinny" flavor. A heavy base means the custard will cook more evenly and is less likely to scorch.

Cooling the custard back down to room temperature so you can get it into the fridge as quickly as possible is just as important as pasteurization to ensure it is safe to eat. The best way to do this is by placing the pan of hot custard in an ice water bath and stirring every few minutes until it cools. This simply means filling a sink or large container with cold water and ice cubes or ice packs. Carefully place the pan upright in the water, making sure that the water level is equal to the level of ice cream base inside—too high and the pan could upturn and too little and it will not cool the mix efficiently. Stir the ice cream base occasionally and once it reaches room temperature, remove from the water bath, cover, and chill in the fridge.

Aging the ice cream base means refrigerating it at 4°C/39°F for at least 4 hours, or preferably overnight. This stage is not absolutely necessary if you are short of time, but I highly recommend it as it produces dramatically better results. Time in the fridge allows the fat molecules to mingle and bond with the water molecules in the recipe. This makes the aged custard mix taste fuller, rounder, and creamier. The ice cream will also hold its shape and have better structure once scooped—making it less "drippy." In any case, the mix should always be fridge-cold before churning, otherwise your ice cream machine will have to work harder to cool it down and it may not freeze sufficiently. There is no need to age sorbet mixes, but these should be chilled before churning.

I like to add the chilled fruit and custard together then liquidize them really well before sieving the mix, to produce a perfectly smooth fake-looking but really

delicious highly aerated soft serve–style result. You can use a stick (or "immersion") blender to do this, or a Vitamix or NutriBullet works brilliantly if you have one, but otherwise a standard upright blender will do the trick. Pour the blended mix into a fine-mesh sieve or chinois (cone-shaped sieve) then use the back of a small ladle to push it through with a plunging action. It might sound fussy to specify what type of sieve to use, but this tip is a chefs' favorite and takes seconds. It is much more efficient than standing around trying to push purée through with a spoon or spatula. The sieved mix can then be poured straight into your ice cream machine and churned.

Aside from the granita, which is still frozen in a freezer, the best way of making the recipes in this book—if you don't have an ice cream machine—is to go out and buy an ice cream machine! They can be bought really cheaply nowadays and will produce a smoother, less icy result than trying to freeze the ice cream yourself.

If you insist on making ice cream without a machine, you can freeze the mixture in a big bowl. After 45 minutes, take it out from the freezer and whisk vigorously. Do this twice, and then consecutively with a big metal spoon or spatula every 30 minutes until uniformly frozen.

In an ice cream machine, churn the mix until it has increased by approximately 20 percent in volume and looks thick and smooth like soft-serve ice cream. If the bowl of the machine has been pre-frozen properly (unless you have a machine with a built-in freezing element) and your mix is cold, this should take about 20 minutes.

The ice cream can be eaten freshly churned—and is extremely good this way, but it will quickly melt! If you are making it to serve later on, then at this point you need to transfer the ice cream quickly into an airtight lidded container. Cover it with a sheet of wax paper (plastic wrap tears when frozen) to avoid exposure to the air before putting the lid on and freezing to harden for at least 4 hours.

Once frozen, recipes will keep well for up to a month, if stored properly, unless stated otherwise. To serve, remove the ice cream from the freezer and place in the fridge for 10 to 15 minutes before scooping. Each recipe makes approximately 1 liter/1 quart, or 10 good scoops.

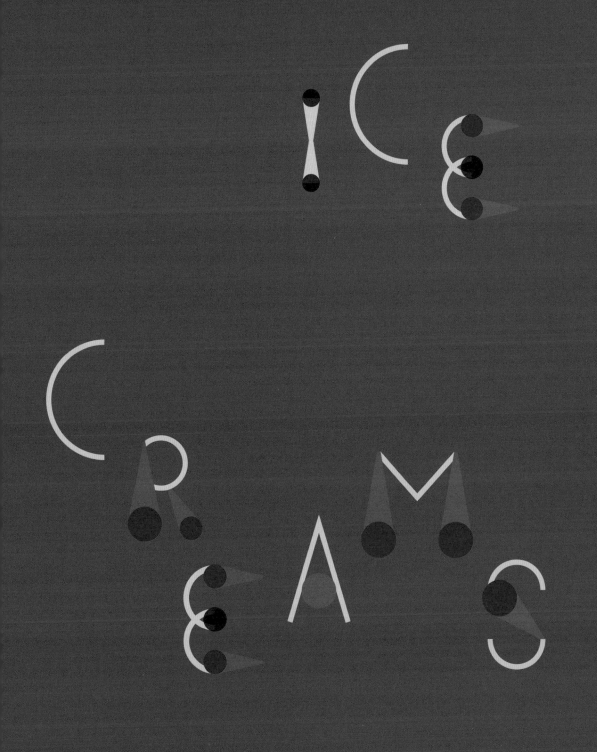

# AMALFI LEMON JELLY

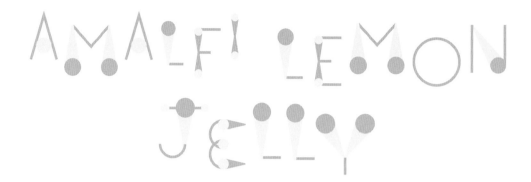

It took a bit of experimentation to create a recipe for lemon ice cream that tasted bright and tangy and smelled as yellow as a just-scratched lemon, but that was also ultra-smooth and creamy. Simmering the lemon juice to reduce its water content, then adding fresh juice and carrageenan (a seaweed-derived gelling agent), makes an intensely lemony jelly. This is blended with zesty custard, resulting—truly—in the ice cream of the gods.

4 large Amalfi lemons or 6 unwaxed lemons
135 g/⅔ cup sugar
Pinch of iota carrageenan (or use powdered gelatin—it will still taste great but won't be quite as smooth)
280 ml/¾ cup whole milk
180 ml/1 cup heavy cream
Small pinch of sea salt
5 egg yolks

1. To make the lemon jelly: wash the lemons then zest and juice them, and strain the juice to remove the seeds. Measure out the lemon juice into two amounts: 200 ml/¾ cup and 50 ml/¼ cup.

2. Put the 200 ml/¾ cup juice in a small non-reactive pan and bring it to a boil. Simmer until the volume of juice is reduced by half. This may take about 10 minutes—keep pouring the juice into a large measuring cup every 4 or 5 minutes to check on its progress and don't let it burn around the edges of the pan. Take care to fully reduce the juice by half as this eliminates water from your ice cream and prevents it from being icy.

3. Put 2 tablespoons of the sugar into a bowl with the carrageenan or gelatin and mix together. Pour in the remaining 50 ml/¼ cup fresh juice and whisk until both the sugar and gelling agent have dissolved.

4. Add the 100 ml/½ cup hot, reduced lemon juice to the gel mix, whisk well, and allow the mixture to cool to a jelly consistency. Cover and chill in the fridge.

5. To prepare the ice cream: heat the milk, cream, and salt together in a non-reactive pan. Stir often, using a whisk or silicone spatula, to prevent it from catching. Once the milk is hot and steaming, whisk the egg yolks and remaining sugar together in a separate bowl to combine.

6. Pour the hot milk in a thin stream over the yolks, whisking continuously. Return the mix to the pan and cook over low heat until it reaches 82°C/180°F, stirring constantly to avoid curdling while making sure it doesn't boil. As soon as your digital thermometer says 82°C/180°F, remove the custard from the heat, whisk in the lemon zest, and place the pan in a sink of ice water to cool it down—you can speed up the process by stirring it every so often. Once the custard is at room temperature, strain it to remove the lemon zest, pour into a clean container, cover with plastic wrap, and chill in the fridge overnight.

7. To make the ice cream: the following day liquidize the cold custard and the lemon jelly together for a couple of minutes until smooth.

8. Pour into an ice cream machine and churn according to the machine's instructions until frozen and the texture of whipped cream, 20 to 25 minutes.

9. Scrape the ice cream into a suitable lidded container. Top with a piece of wax paper to limit exposure to air, cover, and freeze until ready to serve. Best eaten within a fortnight.

Variation—The hard green peel of bergamot fruit is so rich in essential oils that its taste is considered too strong for many culinary uses, but a Bergamot Jelly ice cream has a flavor like a breath of fresh air.

To make the ice cream, take two bergamot, zest one, and juice both. Reserve the zest and measure 100 ml/½ cup juice. Follow the method for the recipe above, but reduce the sugar slightly. This time, don't cook the juice. Mix the carrageenan with 2 tablespoons of the sugar, then whisk in the 100 ml/½ cup fresh bergamot juice to form a gel. Make sure you don't steep the zest in the custard for too long, as it may become bitter.

# Imaginary Neapolitan Ice Cream

Living in Naples in wintertime was annoying, if only because it meant that very few ice cream shops were open. Instead I made do with a *spremuta d'arancia* every couple of days from the *aquafrescaio* at the bottom of Via Toledo.

Draped with bunches of plastic oranges and lemons and situated on one of the most heavily trafficked corners of the city, the kiosk was typical of Naples. This relic of the past served to provide the populace with cold mineral water—the real stuff from underground springs—naturally sulphured and cooled over large blocks of ice. Now it sold cans of San Pellegrino and Peroni, and always glasses of delicious freshly squeezed orange and lemon juice.

The *aquaiuolo* at my local was called Marco. He looked like one half of Right Said Fred and knew pretty much all the local news you needed to know. He told me all about his mother, about how she used to bring a basket of lemons from her parents' garden in the hills above Naples to sell to the former owner of the same kiosk—who used them to flavor the water—until the day when she took over the business herself, eventually handing it over to Marco. He explained how he made lemon granita in the summer using a *grattaghiaccio*—a small box-shaped steel plane, built to slide over the block of frozen lemon syrup and create crystals of shaved ice. I expressed my regret at not being in Naples at the right time of year to try this delicacy, but Marco said I could have his old ice shaver if I wanted... then he thought twice, and said I could have it for 5 euros.

Gelateria della Scimmia (the monkey) was another local hangout—one of the few *gelaterie* that remained open; it was the kind that specialized in huge shiny mounds of ice cream with whole candy bars or pineapples or sometimes toys embedded in them. The kind that most likely relied on foamy packet mixes of flavorings and a heavy hand with the blue food coloring. It sold banana ice cream, shaped on a stick and dipped in chocolate. To be honest these were delicious, and were my treat of choice on a winding walk down from Spaccanapoli to the harbor on my days off. But it was not the kind of ice cream I had fantasized about eating in Naples—the kind of thing you read about in recipe books...

But Naples likes fast food, strong coffee, shiny puffy jackets, wraparound sunglasses, and neon trainers—not lemon leaves and muslin. So I have had to make my own imaginary Neapolitan ice cream—real Neapolitans would rather eat a hot dog and french fry pizza and a frozen banana.

# BUFFALO MILK, ALMOND, AND AMALFI LEMON

The flavor of this ice cream is mild and creamy, just lifted by an oily spritz of lemon. Soften in the fridge for 15 minutes before serving with Espresso Granita (page 211) and Date Shake ice cream (page 209).

100 g/3½ oz whole blanched almonds
1 large Amalfi lemon
140 g/⅔ cup sugar
400 ml/1½ cups buffalo milk or rich, creamy Guernsey milk
3 large egg yolks

1. To prepare the ice cream: place the almonds in a food processor, grate in the zest of the lemon (save the rest of the lemon), and add a couple of tablespoons of the sugar. Pulse them together until fine and gritty, but don't over-grind or the mixture will become oily.

2. Heat the milk in a non-reactive pan, stirring often to prevent it from catching. When the milk is steaming hot, whisk the egg yolks and remaining sugar together in a separate bowl until combined.

3. Pour the hot milk over the yolks in a thin stream, whisking continuously. Return all the mix to the pan and cook over low heat until it reaches 82°C/180°F, stirring all the time to avoid curdling the eggs, while making sure it doesn't boil. As soon as your digital thermometer says 82°C/180°F, remove the pan from the heat, add the ground almonds and stir them in, then cover the pan with plastic wrap and place in a sink of ice water to cool. Once the custard is at room temperature, scrape it into a clean container, cover with plastic wrap, and chill in the fridge.

4. To make the ice cream: the following day, add the juice of the lemon to the custard and blend it for 2 minutes until as smooth as possible.

5. Pour the custard into an ice cream machine and churn according to the machine's instructions until frozen and the texture of whipped cream, 20 to 25 minutes.

6. Scrape the ice cream into a suitable lidded container. Top with a piece of wax paper, cover, and freeze until ready to serve.

# NOVELLINO ORANGE JELLY

Leafy novellino (navel) oranges are found in Italian markets between October and January, and are much prized as eating oranges for their excellent sweet flesh and (by me) for their thick, dusky peel—heavy with fragrant essential oil, which is released with the scratch of a fingernail. I'm not sure whether I love them because I loved scratch 'n' sniff stickers when I was a kid (probable) or I loved scratch 'n' sniff stickers when I was a kid because I loved oranges (doubtful), but I can never resist dragging a fingernail over an orange to have a quick sniff.

This ice cream uses the same method as the Amalfi Lemon Jelly recipe (page 24), with a slight variation in the quantity of juice and sugar used—orange juice is sweeter and more palatable than lemon, after all. The result is much milder and less tart than the lemon ice cream but is softly fragrant and zesty instead, and very lovely.

Serve with Date Shake (page 209) and Saffron Custard ice creams (page 35). It is also delicious sprinkled with some cinnamon-dusted buttery Rye Crumbs (page 160).

3 unwaxed oranges
120 g/⅔ cup sugar
Pinch of iota carrageenan (or use powdered gelatin)
Juice of ½ lemon, strained
160 ml/¾ cup whole milk
300 ml/1 cup heavy cream
Small pinch of sea salt
5 egg yolks

1. To make the orange jelly: rinse the oranges and pat them dry, then zest and juice them. Reserve the zest and strain the juice to remove the seeds. Measure out 250 ml/1 cup juice—if there is any extra, drink it, as you don't need any more for this recipe.

(recipe continues)

2. Place the juice in a small non-reactive pan and bring it to a boil. Simmer until the volume of juice is reduced by half to approximately 120 ml/⅔ cup. This may take about 10 minutes—keep pouring the juice into a large measuring cup every 4 or 5 minutes to check on its progress and really take care not to let it burn around the edges of the pan. Take care to fully reduce the juice by half as this eliminates water from your ice cream and prevents it from being icy.

3. Put 2 tablespoons of the sugar into a bowl with the carrageenan or gelatin and mix together. Whisk the lemon juice into the bowl until the sugar and gelling agent have dissolved.

4. Add the 100 ml/½ cup hot, reduced orange juice to the gel mix, whisk well, and allow to cool to a jelly consistency. Cover and chill in the fridge.

5. To prepare the ice cream: heat the milk, cream, and salt together in a non-reactive pan. Stir often, using a whisk or silicone spatula, to prevent it from catching. Once the milk is hot and steaming, whisk the egg yolks and remaining sugar together in a separate bowl to combine.

6. Pour the hot milk in a thin stream over the yolks, whisking continuously. Return all the mix to the pan and cook over low heat until it reaches 82°C/180°F, stirring all the time to avoid curdling the eggs and keeping a close eye on it so as not to let it boil. As soon as your digital thermometer says 82°C/180°F, remove the custard from the heat, whisk in the orange zest, and place the pan in a sink of ice water to cool it down—you can speed up the cooling process by stirring it every so often. Once the custard is at room temperature, strain it to remove the zest, squeezing hard to extract as much flavor as possible. Pour into a clean container, cover with plastic wrap, and chill overnight.

7. To make the ice cream: the following day, liquidize the custard and orange jelly together for a couple of minutes until perfectly smooth.

8. Pour into an ice cream machine and churn according to the machine's instructions until frozen and the texture of whipped cream, 20 to 25 minutes.

9. Scrape the ice cream into a suitable lidded container. Top with a piece of wax paper to limit exposure to air, cover, and freeze until ready to serve. Best eaten within a fortnight.

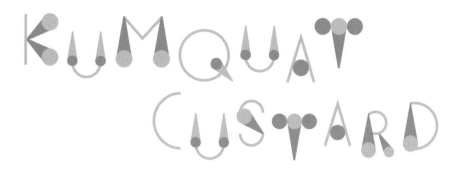

# KUMQUAT CUSTARD

My tiny mind was blown when I first visited Los Angeles—and was greeted by the anti-depressive sight of the January farmers' market with its banks of orange and yellow citrus I'd never even heard of: sweetie-sized mandaquat, Key limes and calamondins, egg-yolk yellow Meyer lemons, and Sunburst tangerines. I snuck half-pound plastic buys of delicate, olive-shaped kumquats into my boots to bring them home with me and experiment with capturing their sweet-and-sour flavor in an ice cream recipe.

I'm not going to demand you start zesting and juicing kumquats to make this ice cream—that sounds like the kind of job you might get asked to do as a bad joke on your first day in a pastry kitchen. The kumquats are cooked whole, as you would for a boiled orange cake, before being blended into the custard base. The resulting ice cream is mild, fragrant, and custardy, with a little chewiness from the pectin you get by using whole fruits. It is brilliant paired with Carrot Seed ice cream (page 34) or Leafy Clementine Granita (page 206).

420 g/1 lb kumquats (or equal weight of thin-skinned citrus fruit)
200 ml/¾ cup whole milk
300 ml/1¼ cups heavy cream
1 tablespoon mild honey
3 egg yolks
210 g/1 cup sugar

1. To prepare the ice cream: wash the kumquats and cook them gently with a tablespoon of water until they are tender. The best way to do this is in a microwave on medium-high for 4 to 5 minutes, as they can't burn. Otherwise, use a pan with a tight-fitting lid to create steam, and cook over medium heat for about 12 minutes, shaking the pan often to make sure they aren't sticking to the bottom. Pierce them with the tip of a sharp knife to check that they're tender. Leave to cool, then chill.

(recipe continues)

2. Heat the milk, cream, and honey together in a non-reactive pan. Stir often to prevent it from catching. Once the liquid is hot and steaming, whisk the egg yolks and sugar together in a separate bowl until combined.

3. Pour the hot liquid in a thin stream over the yolks, whisking continuously. Return all the mix to the pan and cook over low heat until it reaches 82°C/180°F, stirring all the time to avoid curdling the eggs, and keeping a close eye on it so as not to let it boil. As soon as your digital thermometer says 82°C/180°F, place the pan in a sink of ice water to cool it down—you can speed up the cooling process by stirring it every so often. Once the custard is at room temperature, scrape it into a clean container, cover with plastic wrap, and chill in the fridge.

4. To make the ice cream: the following day, add the whole kumquats to the cold custard and liquidize with an immersion blender until as smooth as possible. I mean really blitz them, as you want to get as much kumquat in the mix as possible. Blend until the custard turns a creamy orange color with hardly any flecks of fruit, a good 2 to 3 minutes. Using a small ladle, push the kumquat custard through a fine-mesh sieve or chinois into a clean container.

5. Pour into an ice cream machine and churn according to the machine's instructions until frozen and the texture of whipped cream, 20 to 25 minutes.

6. Scrape the ice cream into a suitable lidded container. Top with a piece of wax paper, cover, and freeze until ready to serve.

Variation—The Meyer lemon is a fragrant, thin-skinned variety of lemon, supposedly a cross between a lemon and a mandarin orange. It has a smooth, orange-tinted peel and a low acidity that once cooked makes it possible to be eaten skin and all—like kumquats. It makes a mild, creamy ice cream that is great when rippled with tangy kumquat or lemon Citrus Gel (see page 223).

To create Meyer Lemon ice cream, cook 2 whole Meyer lemons in a microwave with 100 ml/½ cup of water. Pierce the lemons, place in a bowl covered with plastic wrap, and microwave on high until tender, 5 to 6 minutes. Otherwise, simmer them whole in a pan full of water with a lid on for 45 minutes. Drain and allow to cool before roughly chopping and weighing out 420 g/1 lb fruit then proceeding as above.

# CARROT SEED

This seems like an odd idea until you pinch yourself and remember that many spices—like coriander and pepper—are the seeds of plants. So think of carrot seed as a spice; its wild, aromatic, aniseedy flavor pairs really well with citrus ice creams or fresh strawberries. The reason that it's pretty impractical to use more often in cooking is that the seeds are so tiny—it would take about 2,500 to fill a teaspoon!

You can buy packets of seed from garden centers or online, but if you have a garden and happen to grow carrots, then gathering them yourself in the summer when plants cease flowering, bolt, and "go to seed" is a nice enough way to spend some time—you get tons more than you would from a packet and you end up with fingertips that smell good too.

300 ml/1¼ cups whole milk
300 ml/1¼ cups heavy cream
Pinch of sea salt
110 g/½ cup sugar
5 g/1¼ teaspoon carrot seeds (about 3 packets of seed)
3 egg yolks

1. To prepare the ice cream: heat the milk, cream, and salt in a non-reactive pan. Stir often, using a whisk or silicone spatula, to prevent it from catching.

2. Grind 2 tablespoons of the sugar and the carrot seeds together using a mortar and pestle (failing that, a spice grinder will do). Tip into a bowl with the remaining sugar and egg yolks and whisk until combined.

3. Pour the hot milk and cream over the egg mixture in a thin stream, whisking continuously. Return all the mix to the pan and cook over low heat until it reaches 82°C/180°F, stirring all the time to avoid curdling the eggs, and keeping a close eye on it so as not to let it boil. As soon as your digital thermometer says 82°C/180°F, place the pan into a sink of iced water to cool—stir every so often to help the cooling process along. Once the custard is at room temperature, scrape it into a clean container, cover with plastic wrap, and chill in the fridge.

4. To make the ice cream: the following day, use a small ladle to push the custard through a fine-mesh sieve or chinois into a clean container. Discard any little bits of carrot seed in the sieve and blitz the custard for 1 minute using an immersion or regular blender.

5. Pour the custard into an ice cream machine and churn according to the machine's instructions until frozen and the texture of stiff whipped cream, 20 to 25 minutes.

6. Scrape the ice cream into a suitable lidded container. Top with a piece of wax paper to limit exposure to air, cover, and freeze until ready to serve. Best eaten within a fortnight.

Variations—Substitute the carrot seeds for fresh parsley seed, fennel seed, or dill seed.

Another delicious variation is Saffron Custard. Use the basic custard recipe above (minus the carrot seed) and infuse it with a few threads of saffron overnight (two or three strands max—don't overdo it). Reduce the sugar to 100 g/½ cup and add a teaspoon of light floral honey to make up the sweetness.

# OROBLANCO AND PALE ALE

Oroblanco is a citrus fruit, a hybrid of a seedless white grapefruit and a pomelo. The fruits are large but light, with a thick foamy white pith that tears apart easily to reveal icebergs of sweet, juicy flesh. Their zest is incredibly flavorful and aromatic—and much less bitter than usual grapefruit. Unfortunately, the only place I've found them for sale is in California. On holiday in San Francisco I bought a few pale moon-like fruits from the famous Ferry Plaza farmers' market to put in my rucksack. Back at our motel I lay by the pool, in bliss— drinking ice-cold Sierra Nevada and recording the soft ripping sound of peeling them onto my phone (it was a really good sound).

At the time I was quite pleased with myself for coming up with this flavor combination—but in fact combining grapefruit with pale ale is not much more of a jump from running a cheek of cut lime around the neck of a bottle of beer. Also, when I was a child I'm pretty sure I remember buying lager 'n' lime and cider ice pops from the corner shop…So, as is proven once again, there are no original ideas.

This sorbet is best served from a long paper cup with a slush puppy spoon-straw, and some salty pretzels on the side.

125 g/⅔ cup sugar
125 ml/½ cup water
3 Oroblanco grapefruit, or 2 pink grapefruit and 1 pomelo
200 ml/¾ cup pale ale

1. To prepare the sorbet: heat the sugar and water together in a pan to make a simple syrup, stirring to dissolve the grains of sugar. As soon as the syrup starts to simmer, remove it from the heat. Set aside to cool.

2. Wash the fruit, then pat dry and grate the zest of one fruit directly into the cold simple syrup. Leave this to infuse while you prepare the rest of the sorbet. (Make sure the syrup is cold—infusing grapefruit zest in warm or hot syrup makes it too bitter.)

3. Simmer the pale ale in a non-reactive pan over medium heat until reduced to 100 ml/½ cup. Leave this to cool.

4. Juice all of the fruit. Measure out 400 ml/1½ cups juice and add this to the simple syrup. Stir in the reduced pale ale, and then strain the mix through a fine-mesh sieve to remove the zest. Place in the fridge for at least 2 hours, or until thoroughly chilled.

5. To make the sorbet: once the mix has chilled, give it a good stir and pour it into an ice cream machine, then churn according to the machine's instructions until frozen and the texture of slushy snow, usually 20 to 25 minutes.

6. Scrape the sorbet into a suitable lidded container. Top with a piece of wax paper to limit exposure to air, cover, and freeze until ready to serve. Best eaten within a few days.

Note—The point of simmering the pale ale is to cook off some of the alcohol, while concentrating the flavor. Alcohol has a "melty" effect on sorbets, as it depresses the freezing point, giving the sorbet a softer, more slushy texture. You might notice that this doesn't freeze as hard as the other sorbet recipes, and if left too long in the freezer the alcohol will begin to "weep" from the mix.

# Citrus Tour

Having to take your summer holiday in January (the typical life of the ice cream seller) has its perks, and the color of my perks are orange and yellow!

One winter a few years back, I went on a kind of citrus driving tour of Italy with my little brother Bruno, who—to his credit—kept me company despite never having shown any interest in citrus fruit before, or since.

We flew to Nice and started at the lemon festival in Menton to shop for orange *cédrat*—a warty, medieval-looking type of citron; moving farther along the great damp green Ligurian coast we sought but did not find bitter *chinotti* (chinotto oranges); then we continued on down to Rome to look for the mystical moon-white grapefruits in Giardini Ninfa (closed until April—always check opening times). Further on took us to Sorrento for Amalfi-lemon-everything until we finally ended up in Reggio di Calabria in mid-bergamot season. We found nothing but a strange little bergamot museum (complete with disco-bar—empty in January), a tiny bottle of green bergamot oil in a pharmacy, and a dish of bergamot-flavored boiled sweets in the gas station by the harbor.

On a whim, we took the night ferry over the twinkling straights of Messina to Sicily. Driving into Catania the following morning, we passed Mount Etna and its surrounding frosty orchards lit up with almond blossom, glowing in the low winter sun. Leafy oranges were everywhere in the market and if I expressed my very genuine delight in them, the vendors refused payment and tried to give them away instead—either as a matter of pride or as though they thought they had found a good parent who would love them too.

Cream-filled doughnut-like *zeppole di San Giuseppe* filled the display windows in the Caffé del Duomo, opposite the statue of *u Liotru*—Catania's black lava elephant. The glass-fronted fridges held ice-cold jugs of blood orange juice that had been squeezed so fiercely that they had a thick layer of pink creamy froth on top. It tasted like strawberries and I drank three full glasses, embarrassed to have to keep returning to the cashier to pay my 1 euro 60.

We passed a couple of old guys selling garden lemons out of the trunk of their car. Their cardboard sign read *limone naturale* (non-chemically treated). "*Solo aqua e sapone*," they explained, "*come lei signorita, come lei!*" ("Only washed with soap and water—like you!")

Meanwhile, Bruno got shouted at by a *carabinieri* for dropping orange peel on the pavement. Magic Sicily.

# BLOOD ORANGE AND BERGAMOT SHERBET

A sherbet is like a sorbet but with the addition of a drop of cream to soften it and balance the acidity—although you can leave this out if you prefer. This recipe is a bit like sherbet powder too, frothy and tangy with layers of flavor from the three types of citrus used and an uplifting green fragrance from the bergamot.

155 g/¾ cup sugar
255 ml/1 cup water
3 blood oranges
1 Amalfi or unwaxed lemon
½ green Calabrian bergamot or 1 bergamot lemon
or 3 drops of bergamot oil
Splash of heavy cream

1. To prepare the sherbet: heat the sugar and 155 ml/⅔ cup of the water together in a pan to make a simple syrup, stirring to dissolve the sugar. As soon as the syrup starts to simmer, remove it from the heat. Set aside to cool and then put in the fridge until completely chilled.

2. Zest 1 of the oranges, the lemon, and the bergamot (if using) and scrape the zest into the cold syrup. Juice all of the fruits, then add the juice and remaining 100 ml/½ cup water to the simple syrup and stir well. Chill this mix in the fridge for at least 2 hours.

3. Remove the mix from the fridge, stir in a splash of heavy cream and the bergamot oil (if using), then blitz well with an immersion blender for 1 minute. Strain the mix through a sieve or chinois, squeezing hard to remove the juice from the zest (discard the zest).

4. To make the sherbet: pour the mix into an ice cream machine and churn according to the machine's instructions until frozen and thick and snowy, usually 20 to 25 minutes.

5. Scrape the sherbet into a suitable lidded container. Top with a piece of wax paper to limit exposure to air, cover, and freeze until ready to serve. Best eaten within a fortnight.

# MIMOSA, SEVILLE ORANGE, AND RICE

Walking through the gardens of the American Academy in Rome at 6:30 on a February morning, on my way to do the daily inventory, I would catch fleeting smells in the cold air: mimosa, petitgrain from the bitter orange leaves, artichokes, and (if I crouched right down with nose sniffing the ground) tiny violets.

Mimosa is the real heartbreaker for me, though; it always looks like the sun is shining on it, and seems like a joyful sign from our old pal Mother Nature that spring is on the way.

This ice cream hints at the warm, dry, powdery fragrance of mimosa blossom, and has a confetti of rice and orange peel strewn though its creamy yellow custard base.

20 g/2 tablespoons arborio rice
110 g/½ cup sugar, plus 1 heaping tablespoon
500 ml/2 cups water
Pared zest of 1 Seville orange
300 ml/1¼ cups whole milk
300 ml/1¼ cups heavy cream
Pinch of sea salt
3 egg yolks
50 g/2 oz mimosa blossom
1 heaping tablespoon bitter orange marmalade, finely chopped

1. To make the rice: put the rice, 1 heaping tablespoon of sugar, the water, and long strips of Seville orange zest into a pan and bring to a boil. Simmer until the rice is very tender, about 25 minutes.

2. Drain the rice thoroughly, discarding the strips of orange zest, and spread it out on parchment paper on a platter or baking sheet to cool in a single layer. Once cold, place the platter in the freezer—the reason for doing this is so that the grains of rice freeze individually and not in a big clump. Once the grains are frozen you can scrape them into a zip-top bag and store this in the freezer.

3. To prepare the ice cream: heat the milk, cream, and salt together in a non-reactive pan, stirring often with a whisk or silicone spatula to prevent it from catching. Once the liquid is hot and steaming, whisk the egg yolks and remaining ½ cup sugar together in a separate bowl until combined.

4. Pour the hot milk and cream over the yolks in a thin stream, whisking continuously. Return all the mix to the pan and cook over low heat until it reaches 82°C/180°F, stirring all the time to avoid curdling the eggs, and keeping a close eye on it so as not to let it boil. As soon as your digital thermometer says 82°C/180°F, remove from the heat, add the mimosa blossom, and stir to submerge, then cover the pan with plastic wrap and place into a sink of ice water to cool. Stir every so often to speed the cooling process along. Once the custard is at room temperature, scrape it into a clean container along with the mimosa, cover with plastic wrap, and chill in the fridge.

5. To make the ice cream: the following day, use a small ladle to push the custard through a fine-mesh sieve into a clean container. Squeeze hard to extract as much flavor as possible, then discard the mimosa and blitz the custard for 1 minute using an immersion blender.

6. Pour the custard into an ice cream machine and churn according to the machine's instructions until frozen and the texture of whipped cream, 20 to 25 minutes.

7. Scrape the ice cream into a suitable lidded container, sprinkling in the frozen rice and swirling spoonfuls of chopped marmalade as you go. Top with a piece of wax paper to limit exposure to air, cover, and freeze until ready to serve. Best eaten within a week.

# East Street Market

East Street Market is a long-standing historical place of trade in southeast London, where I have lived for nearly 20 years. It's famous for being cheap and for being situated in quite a dreary location: Elephant and Castle—for years an ignored arse-end of London sliced up by bad town planning, a massive roundabout, a painted pink concrete shopping center, and a whole lot of traffic grinding its way into London from Kent.

One person's eyesore can be another person's eye candy, though, and this market rewards further examination. Among the vendors selling broken biscuits, slippers, and mobile phone chargers, there are stalls selling cheap bowls of overripe or B-grade fruits and vegetables and huge bunches of fresh herbs. It's the place to go if you want to buy a bowl of 20 juicy limes for a pound—just a minute away on the high street you could spend the same amount on three over-packaged rock hard ones.

At the far end of the narrow street is the proprietor of my favorite stall: Mango Man. A man so choosy about his fruit he will go to great pains to select the perfect piece for you to eat that day, likewise the mango that will be perfect in two days time. I don't tell him that the fruit I want is destined for sorbet because I don't think he'd sell it to me . . . it's too precious to be squished. One time, shopping for a bunch of different tropical fruits for a kid's birthday party, I made the mistake of telling him I was making kebabs. His eyes registered an appalled pity I didn't forget for a while . . . Mango Man believes the only way to treat a perfectly ripe fruit is with a squeeze of lime to lift the flavor and balance the sweetness—anything else is somewhat disrespectful.

My dad was a tropical fruit lover too. One of the only pieces of good advice I ever remember him giving me was that the best way to eat a mango is in the bath. When I was small he would sometimes bring home brown paper bags of fruits that were quite exotic for suburban Twickenham and hide them in his bookshelves to ripen. In my memory or perhaps imagination his dusty paperback collection still smells faintly of cigarette ash and guavas. Perhaps this is why I am so fond of Mango Man. In any case, nowadays I have come to agree with them both—which is why there almost wasn't a recipe for mango sorbet . . .

# MANGO

My favorite way to eat mango is to keep it in the fridge before serving, then peel, pit, and slice it perfectly with a sharp knife before drenching it with lime. There's a disclaimer, though, which is that Mango sorbet, sandwiched with Banana, Brown Sugar, and Rum ice cream (page 54) and piled with whipped cream and meringues, is one of the greatest ice cream cakes there is—enough validation for including a recipe here.

155 g/¾ cup sugar
285 ml/1 cup water
2½ small ripe Alphonso or Kesar mangoes
or 3 medium St. Julian mangoes, chilled
2 limes, chilled

1. To prepare the sorbet: first warm the sugar and 155 ml/⅔ cup of the water together in a pan to make a simple syrup. Set aside to cool and then chill in the fridge until needed. (Alternatively, chill the syrup by putting the pan into an ice water bath.)

2. Peel and pit the mangoes and chop the flesh. Weigh out 350 g/12 oz cubed mango flesh and place in a bowl or in a blender.

3. Add the grated zest of the limes, the simple syrup, and remaining ⅓ cup water. Juice the limes, then measure out 90 ml/⅓ cup lime juice and add this to the mango. Liquidize for a minute or two until completely smooth.

4. Using a small ladle, push this mixture through a fine-mesh sieve or chinois. Squeeze hard to extract as much smooth purée as possible. Discard the remaining fibers and zest.

5. To make the sorbet: pour the purée into an ice cream machine and churn according to the machine's instructions until frozen and creamy-looking, usually 20 to 25 minutes.

6. Scrape the sorbet into a suitable lidded container. Top with a piece of wax paper, cover, and freeze until ready to serve.

Note—Using cold mangoes and limes from the fridge means you can churn this sorbet straightaway—it won't require pre-chilling.

# PAPAYA, GREEN CHILE, AND LIME

I love a lot about papaya. It's so good for you—bursting with vitamins and enzymes—I can feel it making me a better person as I eat it. It's also one of my favorite fruits to prepare: laying it lengthwise like a great big beautiful fish and slicing smoothly through its middle to reveal trout-pink insides and a belly of shining seeds like caviar. If only it wasn't for its particular smell—is it just me or does it remind you of baby barf?

Only after a good drenching in acid can you really enjoy papaya properly. A generous squeeze of lime juice and a liberal dose of pungent, freshly grated zest benefit its coolly vegetal, delicate flavor, while erasing the more nauseating aspect of its personality.

This sorbet is super-quick and easy to make, and has a green, refreshing burn from the fresh chile at the end. It should be churned immediately to retain the fresh flavors. Great for breakfast on a hot day, or paired with other sorbets such as Pineapple and Lemongrass (page 48), Passion Fruit Sour (page 46), or Mango (page 43).

175 g/1 cup sugar
175 ml/1 cup water
550 g/1¼ lb ripe papaya (about 1 medium papaya), chilled
3 limes
½ fresh long green chile (a medium-hot variety—not bird's eye!), roughly chopped, with or without seeds
Small pinch of sea salt

44

1. To prepare the sorbet: first warm the sugar and water together in a pan to make a simple syrup. Set aside to cool and then chill in the fridge until needed. (Alternatively, chill the syrup by putting the pan into an ice water bath.)

2. Cut the papaya in half and peel it carefully with a small, sharp knife. Scrape out the seeds and keep these to one side. Cube the flesh and place in a bowl or in a blender.

3. Add the cold syrup to the papaya, then grate the lime zest into the bowl. Juice the limes, measure out 80 ml/⅓ cup juice and add this, the chopped chile, the salt, and a teaspoon of the papaya seeds (see Note).

4. Liquidize really well until the mix seems very smooth, at least 2 minutes. If you are using the papaya seeds, go straight to the next step. Otherwise, use a small ladle to push the purée through a fine-mesh sieve, discarding any fibrous bits or chunks of chile.

5. To make the sorbet: pour the purée straight into an ice cream machine and churn according to the machine's instructions until frozen, thick, and luxurious, usually 20 to 25 minutes.

6. Scrape the sorbet into a suitable lidded container. Top with a piece of wax paper to limit exposure to air, cover, and freeze until ready to serve. Best eaten within a fortnight.

Note—Papaya seeds are edible too, and taste like peppery cress. Adding a spoonful of them to the papaya flesh before liquidizing can add an interesting crunch to the sorbet, and more of a savory flavor.

# PASSION FRUIT SOUR

Passion fruits have a surprise inside! Their crinkly dull skins disguise highly scented, enticing pulp. They are dependable, too—easily available and can be relied upon to yield rich, tropical flavor.

This sorbet is very easy to make and delivers a high-impact sweet 'n' tart flavor. It's a real crowd-pleaser.

180 g/1 cup sugar
200 ml/1 cup water
2 large oranges
8 ripe passion fruit (choose large, deeply wrinkled fruit)

1. To prepare the sorbet: heat the sugar and water together in a pan, stirring to dissolve the grains of sugar. As soon as the syrup starts to simmer, remove it from the heat.

2. Rinse the oranges, then pat dry and grate the zest of one of them directly into the hot syrup. Set aside to cool.

3. Cut the passion fruit in half horizontally and use a teaspoon to scrape the seeds and pulp of each half into a clean bowl. Weigh this—you should have about 180 g/6 oz of pulp.

4. Squeeze the juice of both oranges over the passion fruit and then add the strained cold sugar syrup (discard the zest). Liquidize the lot together for 3 to 4 minutes until the passion fruit seeds have broken down somewhat (leave these in the finished sorbet for texture) and the mixture is frothy and slightly milky-looking. Cover the mixture and put in the fridge until chilled, 2 to 3 hours.

5. To make the sorbet: once cold, whisk the mixture in case it has separated, then pour it into an ice cream machine and churn according to the machine's instructions until thick and frosty-looking, 20 to 25 minutes.

6. Scrape the sorbet into a suitable lidded container. Top with a piece of wax paper to limit exposure to air, cover, and freeze until ready to serve.

Passion Fruit Sour/Papaya, Green Chile, and Lime (page 44)/Pineapple and Lemongrass (page 48)/Mango (page 43)

# PINEAPPLE AND LEMONGRASS

This sorbet deserves its own party. Once churned, it turns the color of 1950s melamine, and the flavor combination is so startling that people's eyes bulge when they taste it.

Inspiration came from traveling with my sister in northern Brazil. We were two little idiotic backpackers—and found ourselves in a hippie town called Lençóis, where the local speciality was carrot pizza. For breakfast in our hostel we were given an otherworldly pineapple juice, flecked with a green leaf I didn't recognize. Further investigation by a local food detective (me) found it had been blended with the blade-like leaves of fresh lemongrass from the garden.

If you don't grow your own lemongrass, then fortunately the shop-bought stalks work as well—just make sure they are fresh.

Choose your pineapple with as much care as you would a friend; sometimes I sniff three or four pineapples before I find the sweetest.

Pineapple contains an enzyme that allows this sorbet to incorporate more air into it than other fruits would while being churned. The results produce a beautiful canary-yellow, creamy sorbet.

Serve it in shot glasses with a splash of tequila or rum, or with rum-soaked *baba* and whipped cream if you want to push the boat out somewhere really tropical.

1 medium pineapple, very ripe (smell it!)
3 lemongrass stalks
180 g/1 cup sugar
180 ml/1 cup water
Zest and juice of 2 limes

1. To prepare the sorbet: slice the top and the bottom away from the pineapple. Stand it upright on its bottom end and remove the rough skin in vertical slices, cutting from top to bottom. Don't worry if some little "eyes" remain—these will be sieved away later.

2. Following the central line of its core (again from top to bottom), cut the pineapple into four pieces, then remove the lengths of core from each quarter and keep them to one side. Starting with the flower end (see page 18) cube the pineapple flesh and weigh out exactly 560 g/20 oz (or 1½ lb); place this in a bowl or in a blender.

3. Using a sharp, heavy knife, finely chop the lemongrass. Use the whole stalk, but please be careful of your fingertips.

4. Add the sugar, water, pineapple cores (not the cubed flesh), and lemongrass to a pan and bring to a simmer, stirring carefully to dissolve the sugar. Remove from the heat, cover, and leave the syrup to cool in an ice water bath.

5. Pick the pineapple cores out of the syrup and discard (although these are yummy to chew on). Add the lime zest and juice and the syrup to the pineapple cubes, and leave to macerate in the fridge for 3 hours, until completely cold.

6. To make the sorbet: remove the mixture from the fridge and blitz very thoroughly for a minute or two. Push the mixture through a fine-mesh sieve, squeezing to extract as much flavor as possible from the fibrous bits. Pour into an ice cream machine and churn according to the machine's instructions until frozen, billowy, and creamy-looking, usually 20 to 25 minutes.

7. Transfer the sorbet into a suitable lidded container. Top with a piece of wax paper to limit exposure to air, cover, and freeze until ready to serve.

# GUAVA AND SUGARCANE

Ice cream in Brazil is called *sorvete* (pronounced "sore-ve-chee") and comes in a misty tropical rainbow of colors, mirroring the unbelievable range of delicious ripe fruit that is available. It's also really fun to buy: your flavor of choice is scooped onto little scales and sold by weight—a nice touch evoking gemstones, gold, "pharmaceuticals," and equally precious goods.

Brazilian ice creams are sometimes water-based like regular sorbet—only thickened with tapioca starch so they don't melt too quickly in the heat. Otherwise (because fresh dairy is difficult to come by), fruit is mixed with condensed milk and *crème de leite*—a thin ultra-pasteurized cream commonly available tinned or in cartons.

As well as the more unusual indigenous fruits—like the tiny, juicy *siriguela*, which has thin edible skin and sour mango-like insides, and *jabuticaba*, which could best be described as a big, crunchy, peppery blackcurrant from outer space, my go-to choice was always flowery flavored, granular guava.

For this sorbet, guava is blended with rapadura sugar—the taste reminds me of the rich flavor of cachaça, a Brazilian alcohol distilled from sugarcane that forms the basis of drinks like *caipirinha*—and lime, and it's a pretty irresistible combination. Softest pale pink and almost alarmingly aromatic, with a texture somewhere between coconut ice and fudge, it's an evocative taste of the tropics.

250 ml/1 cup water

130 g/¾ cup rapadura whole cane sugar or coconut sugar (available from most health food shops)

4 ripe guavas (about 450 g/1 lb total weight)

Zest and juice of 2 limes

1. To prepare the sorbet: heat the water and the rapadura sugar together in a small non-reactive pan over low heat. Stir to dissolve the grains of sugar and bring to a simmer.

2. Rinse the guavas, then slice away the flower and stem ends before roughly chopping the fruit into medium chunks. Add this to the warm cane syrup along with any juice.

3. Simmer the fruit very gently until the guava is opaque and perfectly tender, 4 to 5 minutes; remove from the heat. Stir in the grated lime zest and set aside to cool. Once cold, cover and refrigerate for 2 to 3 hours (or overnight) until chilled.

4. To make the sorbet: add the lime juice to the cold guava and blend the whole lot with an immersion blender until as smooth as possible. Push the purée through a fine-mesh sieve or chinois to remove the many rock-hard seeds.

5. Pour the purée into an ice cream machine and churn according to the machine's instructions until frozen and thick and snowy, usually 20 to 25 minutes.

6. Transfer the sorbet to a suitable lidded container. Top with a piece of wax paper to limit exposure to air, cover, and freeze until ready to serve.

Note—Guavas are at their best when they are very ripe. Let them sit at room temperature in the kitchen for a few days, or until the fruit smells very pungent and yields to gentle pressure from your fingers.

# TAMARILLO

Tropical fruits are an old-fashioned embodiment of real luxury to me, and tamarillo is a quintessential tropical fruit. Strange and wondrous, it shares the pungency of guava and the sharpness of passion fruit with a hint of raw tomato. Look for really ripe squashy ones in ethnic markets. The sumptuous orchid-colored ice cream they produce really is rather special.

150 ml/½ cup whole milk
250 ml/1 cup heavy cream
3 large egg yolks
160 g/¾ cup sugar
550 g/19 oz very ripe tamarillo

1. To prepare the ice cream: heat the milk and cream together in a non-reactive pan. Stir often, using a whisk or silicone spatula, to prevent it from catching. When the milk is hot and steaming, whisk the egg yolks and sugar together in a separate bowl until combined.

2. As the liquid reaches the simmering point, pour it in a thin stream over the yolks, whisking constantly. Make sure the yolks are well combined with the liquid, then return all the mix to the pan and cook over low heat until it reaches 82°C/180°F. Stir constantly to avoid curdling the eggs and keep a close eye on it so as not to let it boil. As soon as your digital thermometer says 82°C/180°F, place the pan of custard in a sink of ice water and leave to cool, stirring occasionally, to speed up the cooling process. Once the custard is at room temperature, cover with plastic wrap and chill in the fridge overnight, or for at least 8 hours.

3. To make the ice cream: halve the tamarillo and, using a spoon, scrape out the ripe flesh into a bowl or the jug of a blender. Add the cold custard and liquidize both parts together until very smooth, 2 to 3 minutes. Use a small ladle to push the purée through a fine-mesh sieve or chinois and remove the seeds.

4. Pour the custard into an ice cream machine and churn according to the machine's instructions until thick and frozen and the texture of whipped cream, usually 20 to 25 minutes.

5. Transfer the ice cream to a suitable lidded container. Top with a piece of wax paper, cover, and freeze until ready to serve.

# BANANA, BROWN SUGAR, AND RUM

The world's best banana ice cream is from Argentina, where pretty much all ice creams are based upon *dulce de leche*—a kind of soft toffee made from the long condensing of milk and sugar. Condensed milk is used heavily in ice cream production in South American countries, as fresh cream is difficult to come by. Dulce de leche lasts forever, has more than twice the protein of milk, and works wonders on the texture of ice cream—giving it a hint of saltiness, great structure, and "chew." A perfect match for banana!

Nowadays my preference is for less sweet ice creams, so I've given two options for the recipe below. Made with dulce de leche the ice cream is slightly more caramelized; the other, using muscovado sugar, tastes moderately "cleaner." Both are over-the-top banana and totally delicious. Have faith in putty-colored ice creams.

2 very ripe medium bananas
2 tablespoons dark rum
2 heaping tablespoons dulce de leche
or 25 g/2 tablespoons muscovado sugar
150 ml/½ cup whole milk
250 ml/1 cup heavy cream
Pinch of sea salt
2 egg yolks
85 g/½ cup sugar

1. To prepare the ice cream: slice the bananas thinly into a pan, add the rum and either dulce de leche or muscovado sugar, and heat over medium heat until the bananas collapse and the sugars melt and start bubbling, stirring constantly. Allow it to bubble gently for about 10 minutes to cook the alcohol off, then scrape the contents into a bowl and cool before chilling in the fridge.

2. Heat the milk, cream, and salt together in a non-reactive pan. Stir often, using a whisk or silicone spatula, to prevent it from catching. Once the milk is hot and steaming, whisk the egg yolks and sugar together in a separate bowl until combined.

3. Pour the hot milk in a thin stream over the yolks, whisking continuously. Return all the mix to the pan and cook over low heat until it reaches 82°C/180°F, stirring all the time to avoid curdling the eggs and keeping a close eye on it so as not to let it boil. As soon as your digital thermometer says 82°C/180°F, place the pan in a sink of ice water to cool it down—speed up the cooling process by stirring it every so often. Once the custard is at room temperature, pour it into a clean container, cover with plastic wrap, and chill in the fridge.

4. To make the ice cream: the following day, add the chilled banana mix to the cold custard and liquidize with an immersion blender until as smooth as possible. Using a small ladle, push the banana custard through a fine-mesh sieve or chinois into a clean container to remove any remaining lumps.

5. Pour into an ice cream machine and churn according to the machine's instructions until frozen and the texture of whipped cream, usually 20 to 25 minutes.

6. Scrape the ice cream into a suitable lidded container. Top with a piece of wax paper to limit exposure to air, cover, and freeze until ready to serve.

Note—The dulce de leche version is very good with a handful of chopped raw walnuts sprinkled in at the end, too.

# Italian Kiwi

In Rome, on the 14th of February (also known as *La Festa di San Valentino)* there is not a strawberry—let alone a chocolate-dipped strawberry—in sight. Instead the *fruttivendolo* displays trays of friendly-looking brown kiwi fruit, and *caffè* windows are piled high with bright oranges.

In 2007, when I worked at the American Academy in Rome, I had a boyfriend—a beautiful rock musician who wore high heels. We met in Piazza Santa Maria in Trastevere on Valentine's Day and he gave me a box of kiwi fruit, then we kissed and drank freshly squeezed blood orange juice mixed with Campari.

I proceeded to eat peeled kiwi fruit every day for breakfast until I got gingivitis from the acidity and my gums started bleeding and I had to run, crying in pain, to the hospital in the middle of the night. In the completely deserted wards of the Ospedale Fatebenefratelli on the Isola Tiberina, I had my mouth inspected by a lone doctor wearing a cowboy hat and cowboy boots under his scrubs. He was listening to the Pet Shop Boys on a loud Walkman. My mouth was so sore I could not eat or drink for four days, and it had to be treated with silver nitrate. My boss, Mona, did not hide her deep suspicion that I caught something from my boyfriend and would not come within six feet of me. I slowly recovered, and began to be able to sip raw egg and Marsala milkshakes at Pascucci's on Via di Torre Argentina.

The only moral of this story is that sometimes Italy is too much and I try to guzzle it all in too quickly, but—with a kiwi at least—a warning that a little moderation is a good thing.

I always assumed kiwi fruits were subtropical, and was surprised to see so many in Rome. It turns out that in the 1930s Mussolini had the swampy soil around Lazio drained to create new farmland and "encouraged" everybody to grow them; they took to the new sandy soil surprisingly well. Italy is now the world's biggest producer of kiwi fruit!

# KIWI

If you want to preserve the bright green color of the fruits in this sorbet, you can make it using white sugar. Another tip for retaining the color is to churn the sorbet immediately after making. Use chilled kiwi fruit straight from the fridge so your mix is already cold when you pour it into the ice cream machine.

The best pairing for this sherberty lip-smacking sorbet is a rice ice cream, made using the recipe on page 40 but flavored with ground cinnamon (the mimosa and marmalade left out). The soft, milky nuggets offset the sorbet's bracing green sourness nicely.

100 g/½ cup sugar
100 ml/½ cup water
700 g/1½ lb firm, ripe kiwi fruit, chilled
Juice of 1 lemon or lime

1. To prepare the sorbet: heat the sugar and water together in a pan to make a simple syrup, stirring to dissolve the grains of sugar. As soon as the syrup starts to simmer, remove it from the heat. Set aside to cool, then chill in the fridge until completely cold.

2. Top and tail the kiwi and cut away the woody bit at the stem end. Stand the halves cut-side down on a chopping board and cut away the furry skin, removing as little flesh as possible. Slice into quarters.

3. Liquidize the kiwi quarters with the lemon juice and the cold simple syrup. Use a small ladle to push the purée through a fine-mesh sieve or chinois. Save a couple of tablespoons of the seeds and add these back to the purée. (Don't be tempted to skip the sieving, though; otherwise the sorbet will end up looking gray.)

4. To make the sorbet: pour the frog-green purée into an ice cream machine and churn according to the machine's instructions until frozen and thick and creamy-looking, usually 20 to 25 minutes.

5. Transfer the sorbet to a suitable lidded container. Top with a piece of wax paper, cover, and freeze until ready to serve.

# RHUBARB AND RASPBERRY RIPPLE

This ice cream is prettiest when made with the slim stalks of forced rhubarb from Yorkshire's magic "Rhubarb Triangle." The candy-pink sticks transform into clouds of ice cream the color of bubblegum.

There's more to this ice cream than just retro appeal. The light, earthy flavor of the rhubarb is set off with a tart twist of raspberry syrup.

150 g/¾ cup frozen raspberries
220 g/1 cup sugar
500 g/1 lb rhubarb
Zest and juice of 1 orange
150 ml/½ cup whole milk
200 ml/1 cup heavy cream
Pinch of sea salt
3 egg yolks

1. To make the raspberry syrup: if you have a microwave, put the berries into a heatproof bowl with 60 g/¼ cup of the sugar and simply blast them for a minute or two, or until the fruit is very lightly cooked. Otherwise put into a pan with a tablespoon of water and simmer just until the raspberries soften and collapse and the sugar dissolves.

2. Once cooked, leave the berries to cool, then blitz them with an immersion blender. Push the purée through a sieve to remove the seeds, squeezing hard to extract as much fruit as possible. Save the seeds for pip juice (see page 18), let the syrup cool, and then chill it in the fridge overnight (which will thicken the syrup considerably).

3. To make the rhubarb: rinse the rhubarb, top and tail the stalks, then slice into 3 cm/1-inch-long pieces and place these into a non-reactive pan or heatproof bowl and add the orange zest and juice. Cook very gently until the fruit collapses, either on the stove, or in a microwave.

(recipe continues)

If using a pan, keep a lid on and shake the pan every so often to prevent it from sticking. It should take 10 to 15 minutes, or 2 to 3 minutes covered with plastic wrap in a microwave. Try to avoid boiling the rhubarb, as with a sudden "ploof!" it will quickly become pale stewed mush. Leave to cool completely and then chill in the fridge.

4. To prepare the ice cream: heat the milk, cream, and salt together in a non-reactive pan. Stir often, using a whisk or silicone spatula, to prevent it from catching. When the milk is hot, whisk the egg yolks and remaining 160 g/¾ cup sugar together until combined.

5. As the milk reaches the simmering point, pour it in a thin stream over the yolks, whisking all the time. Return all the mix to the pan and cook over low heat until it reaches 82°C/180°F, stirring constantly to avoid curdling the eggs; keep a close eye on it so as not to let it boil. As soon as your digital thermometer says 82°C/180°F, remove the pan from the heat and place in a sink of ice water to cool—you can speed up the cooling process by stirring it every so often. Once the custard is at room temperature, cover with plastic wrap and chill in the fridge.

6. To make the ice cream: add the chilled rhubarb to the cold custard and liquidize until absolutely smooth, 2 to 3 minutes. Push the rhubarb custard through a fine-mesh sieve or chinois into a clean container, discarding any leftover fibers.

7. Pour into an ice cream machine and churn according to the machine's instructions until frozen and the texture of whipped cream, 20 to 25 minutes.

8. Working quickly, transfer the ice cream into a suitable lidded container. Do this in layers, adding a generous layer of chilled raspberry syrup each time, then swirling with a spoon for a marbled effect. Top with a piece of wax paper to limit exposure to air, cover, and freeze until ready to serve.

Note—Cooked rhubarb always benefits from sitting in the fridge overnight... it seems to intensify and draw out the beautiful pink juice.

# BLACKCURRANT LEAF WATER ICE

Trying the flavor of blackcurrant leaves for the first time is almost like finding out that a new color exists (see Leafy Blackcurrant Custard, page 110). It's a singular perfume... a bit like tart hard candy... a bit like green leaves... reminiscent of exciting chemicals.

If this sounds weird, don't let it put you off. It's delicious enough to be up there as a fourth flavor—strawberry, chocolate, and vanilla pale in comparison.

200 g/1 cup sugar
420 ml/1⅔ cups water
30 g/1 cup blackcurrant leaf tips, freshly picked and rinsed
(or see Variation, page 63)
4 lemons, ideally unwaxed Amalfi

1. To prepare the water ice: gently heat the sugar and water together in a small pan to make a syrup, stirring until the sugar has dissolved. Bring this syrup to a simmer, then remove it from the heat and add the blackcurrant leaves. Cover the pan with plastic wrap and leave the syrup to cool in an ice water bath for about half an hour.

2. Zest and juice the lemons. Measure out 250 ml/1 cup of the juice (I'm sure you'll find something to do with any that's left over), then add this and the zest to the cool syrup. Stir then strain through a fine-mesh sieve, squeezing to extract as much liquid as possible from the blackcurrant leaves. Chill in the fridge.

3. To make the water ice: once the mix is chilled, give it a good stir and then pour into an ice cream machine and churn according to the machine's instructions until frozen and the texture of slushy snow, usually 20 to 25 minutes.

(recipe continues)

4. Scrape the water ice into a suitable lidded container. Top with a piece of wax paper to limit exposure to air, cover, and freeze until ready to serve.

Note—This is a water ice rather than a sorbet, as it doesn't have the "body" provided by a fruit purée. It will naturally be icy and a little "melty," but intensely refreshing.

Variation—Make a deliciously refreshing Bunch of Fresh Herbs sorbet by replacing the blackcurrant leaves with 30 g/2 tablespoons fresh soft green herbs or blossoms of your choice. I like to experiment with dill, parsley, basil, chervil, mint, or anise hyssop. Even a few honey-suckle, calendula, or sweet pea blossoms make a nice addition (maybe not chives). Chop them up finely and add to the hot sugar syrup, then steep for 20 minutes in an ice bath before straining out and proceeding as above.

Alternatively, omit the blackcurrant leaves entirely and follow the method above to make a classic lemon sorbet. It's nice to add the fresh zest of 1 lemon to the mix before churning for visual appeal—otherwise real lemon sorbet has the misfortune to look like mashed potatoes.

# PEACH LEAF MILK ICE

Peach leaves appear to be completely flavorless until they are scalded in hot milk for a very specific amount of time (see Note). At this point they deliver their extraordinary hidden characteristic—the flavor of crisp toasted almond biscuits. Wow your party guests by live demo-ing this ice cream for them. Wow yourself every time you make it at home!

Getting ahold of the leaves may prove tricky—I buy bags of them from a stall at Brixton farmers' market, where amazingly a few small knobby (and slightly green) Sussex-grown peaches are sold each summer. Or find your own tree: peach trees are notoriously difficult to bear fruit, but if you find someone who has a tree they are unlikely to miss a dozen or so leaves if you ask nicely.

This recipe employs the use of a simple milk base, thickened with natural vegetable starch so as not to interfere with the pure taste of peach leaf. A surprising and refreshing ice, delicious with a side of lightly sugared, sliced stone fruit.

160 g/¾ cup sugar
15 g/1 tablespoon tapioca starch or cornstarch
500 ml/2 cups whole milk
150 ml/¾ cup heavy cream
15 to 20 fresh peach leaves (or see Variations, opposite)

1. To prepare the milk ice: prepare a sink full of ice water, and set a timer to 3 minutes. Have a clean bowl ready with a fine-mesh sieve set over it. In a bowl, whisk 2 tablespoons of the sugar into the tapioca starch or cornstarch.

2. Heat the remaining sugar with the milk and cream in a pan over low heat, stirring often with a whisk or silicone spatula to prevent it from catching. Once the liquid is hot and steaming, pour it into the bowl containing the starch. Whisk constantly to combine it well without lumps forming.

3. Return all the mix to the pan and cook it over low heat, whisking constantly, just until it starts to simmer. Remove the pan from the heat, stir in the peach leaves, then cover the pan tightly with plastic wrap and place it in the sink full of ice water to cool. Start the timer.

4. After exactly 3 minutes remove the pan and pour the mix through the sieve. Squeeze hard to extract as much flavor as possible from the peach leaves. You should see a tint of pale acid green seep into the mix with the last squeezes. Discard the remaining leaves.

5. Return the pan to the sink to cool completely before covering and chilling in the fridge overnight.

6. To make the milk ice: the following day, liquidize the peach leaf mixture with an immersion blender for 1 minute to help liquefy the mix.

7. Pour the mix into an ice cream machine. Churn according to the machine's instructions until frozen and the texture of whipped cream, 20 to 25 minutes.

8. Scrape the milk ice into a suitable lidded container. Top with a piece of wax paper to limit exposure to air, cover, and freeze until ready to serve. This ice will keep for a few days, but is best eaten right away—as the recipe contains no egg yolk and very little cream, it freezes quite hard and can become icy otherwise.

Note—It's vital that you use a timer for this so the peach leaves are steeped for no more than 3 minutes precisely—any longer and the flavor changes completely to that of overripe compost.

Variations—Make a clean and pure-tasting Fig Leaf Milk Ice by following the recipe above and replacing the peach leaves with 2 large or 3 small fresh fig leaves.

Make Pea Pod Milk Ice by simmering 350 g/¾ lb shelled pea pods for 3 to 4 minutes in the milk and cream mixture (before you add the starch), then blitz with an immersion blender and strain before returning the mix to a clean pan. Bring to a steaming point and then pour over the starch in the bowl and continue as above.

# PIGEON FIG AND PINEAU DES CHARENTES

In Puglian dialect this variety of fig is known as *culummi bianchi* (from the Italian word for dove—*colomba*), because of their resemblance to the fat baby doves or pigeons that are known for their habit of plopping out of trees in springtime. This fruit is born from the first flowering of the tree and it signals the beginning of the fig season.

Pigeon figs, or *ficione*, have pale, waxy green skins that look as though they were made of painted marzipan, and fresh pink insides—a lot less sweet than the stickier *settembrini* fig and other late summer varieties. By virtue of their tender skins, they can be eaten whole. I love their cool, fresh, rainy flavor, and set it off with a rich, eggy custard base and the light pine-y addition of Pineau—a young, fortified wine aperitif made from grape must and Cognac. Very fancy served next to Green Walnut ice cream (page 144) and Fig Leaf and Raspberry sorbet (page 141).

500 g/1 lb first flower figs (use tinned green figs if you cannot find them, and rinse the syrup off first)
150 ml/½ cup whole milk
250 ml/1 cup heavy cream
3 egg yolks
135 g/⅔ cup sugar
50 ml/¼ cup Pineau des Charentes

1. To prepare the ice cream: check the figs over, rinse if necessary and trim away the very tops of their stalks (if attached).

2. Cook the whole figs very gently with a couple of tablespoons of water until they are tender. The best way to do this is in a microwave

on medium-high for 4 to 5 minutes, as they can't burn. Otherwise use a pan with a tight-fitting lid to create steam, and cook over medium-low heat for about 12 minutes, shaking the pan often to make sure they aren't sticking to the bottom. Pierce them with the tip of a sharp knife to check that they're tender and piping hot all the way through. Leave to cool, then chill in the fridge.

3. Heat the milk and cream together in a non-reactive pan, stirring often with a whisk or silicone spatula to prevent it from catching. Once the liquid is hot and steaming, whisk the egg yolks and sugar together in a separate bowl until combined.

4. Pour the hot liquid over the yolks in a thin stream, whisking continuously. Return all the mix to the pan and cook over low heat until it reaches 82°C/180°F, stirring all the time to avoid curdling the eggs, and keeping a close eye on it so as not to let it boil. As soon as your digital thermometer says 82°C/180°F, place the pan in a sink of ice water to cool—you can speed up the cooling process by stirring it every so often. Once the custard is at room temperature, scrape it into a clean container, cover with plastic wrap, and chill in the fridge.

5. To make the ice cream: the following day, add the whole figs and the Pineau to the cold custard and liquidize with an immersion blender until as smooth as possible. Blend until the custard turns a creamy pale yellow, 2 to 3 minutes. Using a small ladle, push the fig custard through a fine-mesh sieve or chinois into a clean container.

6. Pour into an ice cream machine and churn until frozen and the texture of whipped cream, 20 to 25 minutes.

7. Scrape the ice cream into a suitable lidded container. Top with a piece of wax paper to limit exposure to air, cover, and freeze until ready to serve.

Variation—Make a rich, dusky Black Fig and Marsala ice cream in the autumn using sweeter purple Turkish or *settembrini* figs, and blending them with a zabaglione-flavored custard made with Marsala. Follow the recipe above and substitute the Pineau for a good dry Marsala.

# RHUBARB AND ANGELICA

Cooling angelica grows both wild and cultivated and can be harvested in May—by happy coincidence at just the same time that robust sticks of garden rhubarb are ready to pull from the damp spring soil. This leafy herb looks a bit like overgrown celery; it has a large flower head containing masses of aromatic seeds. Crush the long, hollow stalks to release the fresh medicinal odor (you might recognize it as being the main flavoring in chartreuse).

Verjuice (an acidic juice, made from pressed unripe grapes) brings clarity to this sorbet recipe and helps contribute a pleasing balance of sweet and sour. A perfect after-dinner sorbet: just keep tasting the syrup so it doesn't get too strong, as a little goes a long way and it can start to smell like boiled peas if cooked too long. Delicious paired with Gariguette Strawberry ice cream (page 77).

550 g/1¼ lb rhubarb
1 orange
120 g/½ cup fresh angelica (about 1 stem, 30 cm/1 inch long)
200 g/1 cup sugar
200 ml/1 cup water
75 ml/⅓ cup verjuice or lemon juice

1. To prepare the sorbet: rinse the rhubarb, top and tail the stalks, then slice into 3 cm/1-inch-long pieces. Place in a non-reactive pan or an ovenproof dish. Add a tablespoon of water and the zest and juice of the orange. Cover the pan with a lid (or if using an oven dish use tight-fitting foil). Cook on the stove over very gentle heat for about

(recipe continues)

20 minutes or in an oven preheated to 300°F for about 25 minutes until the rhubarb is tender. If using a pan, hold the lid tight and shake it gently every so often to prevent it from sticking. Once cooked, leave to cool completely and then cover and chill in the fridge overnight.

2. Trim any leaves from the stem of angelica. These are bitter and will spoil the flavor of the syrup. Slice the hollow stems into 1 cm/½-inch lengths.

3. Heat the sugar and water together in a pan over low heat, stirring to dissolve the grains of sugar. As the syrup reaches the simmering point, toss in the angelica. Remove from the heat, cover the pan with a lid or with plastic wrap, and place in a sink of ice water to cool. Take care not to boil the angelica syrup—it tastes like boiled peas if cooked too long. Once the syrup reaches room temperature place in the fridge to chill completely.

4. To make the sorbet: strain the angelica syrup over the rhubarb, discarding the leftover angelica. Add the verjuice and blend the rhubarb with an immersion blender until absolutely smooth. Push the purée through a fine-mesh sieve or chinois into a clean container. Squeeze hard to extract as much purée as possible.

5. Pour into an ice cream machine and churn according to the machine's instructions until thick, creamy, and frozen, about 20 minutes.

6. Transfer the sorbet to a suitable lidded container. Top with a piece of wax paper to limit exposure to air, cover, and freeze until ready to serve.

Note—The width of angelica stems can vary hugely (especially if you pick them in the wild) from the root end, which can have the diameter of a roll of tape, to the pencil-slim tips. Select a length of the stalk just where it starts to become hollow. The wider parts are good for candying but the flavor would overwhelm this sorbet.

# MONTMORENCY CHERRY SHERBET

Fresh cherries are a treat to eat—sweet and sharp and juicy, with taut shiny skins that crack as you bite into them. But their flavor is hard to distinguish UNLESS they are of a sour variety. Don't spoil beautiful ripe cherries by turning them into ice cream or sorbet. No matter how tenderly you treat them, your efforts will be wasted. Hold out to make Montmorency Cherry Sherbet instead.

If you can get hold of a Montmorency (or Griotte) cherry to take a bite, you'll find it mouth-puckeringly sour and wretched. Only lightly cooking the fruit brings out the intense flavor you recognize from classic cherry candy or Cherry Coke. They taste fake!

Likewise, morello cherries are so clear and bright with such a plucky flavor; try contacting pick-your-own farms to seek them out.

This recipe constitutes a sherbet because of the addition of a splash of fresh cream—just enough to soften the sharpness. It's the perfect recipe to serve blended with ice-cold Prosecco to make a *sgroppino* cocktail—especially if you can find a succulent Luxardo maraschino cocktail cherry to top it with.

450 g/1 lb Montmorency or morello cherries, pits in
150 g/¾ cup sugar
100 ml/½ cup water
Zest and juice of 1 unwaxed or Amalfi lemon
Splash of heavy cream
1 tablespoon Luxardo maraschino liqueur (optional)

(recipe continues)

1. To prepare the sherbet: leaving the pits in, lightly cook the cherries with the sugar and water. If you have a microwave, zap them in a heat-proof bowl for 4 to 5 minutes on high, until the fruit is lightly cooked. If not, cook it all in a small non-reactive pan just until the cherries burst and are piping hot. Allow to cool to room temperature.

2. Once the cherries are cool enough to handle, wash your hands and pit each one carefully using your fingers. Place the cherries and their syrup in a blender along with the lemon zest and juice, cream, and liqueur (if using). Liquidize until very smooth, 2 to 3 minutes. Use the back of a small ladle to push the mix through a fine-mesh sieve or chinois. Cover the purée and chill in the fridge until completely cold, 2 to 3 hours.

3. To make the sherbet: pour the cherry purée into an ice cream machine and churn according to the machine's instructions until frozen and thick and creamy-looking, usually 20 to 25 minutes.

4. Scrape the sherbet into a suitable lidded container. Top with a piece of wax paper to limit exposure to air, cover, and freeze until ready to serve.

Note—I like to cook cherries with their pits in, and pit them after-ward. Just like cooking beef on the bone, it adds flavor—except it is a nicer, more almondy flavor!

PEA POD

In 2009 I was asked to make an ice cream to sell at the Art Car Boot Fair in London's Bethnal Green. The theme that year was "recession special." There were a lot of "credit crunchy" kinds of flavors going on among cake bakers, but I wanted to try and make a cheap milk ice out of pea pods (pods are popping with sweet fresh flavor but are usually thrown away, and that seems a shame to waste). I billed it as 100 pence ice cream and sold scoops for a pound a pop. It went down a storm and I still make it now in the summer—albeit a slightly more costly custard version. It's delightful served with fresh strawberries or Gariguette Strawberry ice cream (page 77) on the side, and a sprinkle of sea salt flakes.

400 g/1 lb very fresh peas in their pods
300 ml/1¼ cups whole milk
250 ml/1 cup heavy cream
Small pinch of sea salt
4 egg yolks
130 g/⅔ cup sugar

1. To prepare the ice cream: wash the peas in their pods and then shell them, reserving the pods. Blanch the fresh podded peas in boiling water for 30 seconds and then refresh them in ice water to preserve their color; drain and put them in the fridge, covered.

2. Heat the milk, cream, and salt together, stirring occasionally. As soon as the liquid reaches the simmering point, add the pea pods and simmer them for 3 minutes. Remove the pan from the heat and blitz the pods and liquid with an immersion blender for a minute. Strain the mixture through a sieve, squeezing hard on the pods to extract as much flavor from them as possible. Discard the blitzed pea pods.

3. Wash the pan and pour the fragrant milk and cream mixture back into it. Bring to a simmer. Stir often, using a whisk or silicone spatula, to prevent it from catching. Once the liquid is hot and steaming, whisk the egg yolks and the sugar together in a separate bowl until combined.

4. Pour the hot liquid over the yolks in a thin stream, whisking continuously. Return all the mix to the pan and cook over low heat until it reaches 82°C/180°F. Stir constantly to avoid curdling the eggs, and keep a close eye on it so as not to let it boil. As soon as your digital thermometer says 82°C/180°F, place the pan in a sink of ice water to cool. Speed up the cooling process by stirring the mix every so often. Once the custard is at room temperature, scrape it into a clean container, cover with plastic wrap, and chill in the fridge overnight.

5. To make the ice cream: the following day, add the blanched peas to the custard and liquidize with an immersion blender until it turns froggy green, 2 minutes. Use a small ladle to push the mixture through a fine-mesh sieve to ensure it is perfectly smooth.

6. Pour the custard into an ice cream machine. Churn according to the machine's instructions until frozen and the texture of whipped cream, usually 20 to 25 minutes.

7. Scrape the ice cream into a suitable lidded container. Top with a piece of wax paper to limit exposure to air, cover, and freeze until ready to serve. Eat within a week.

# GARIGUETTE STRAWBERRY

Strawberry is a famous yet forgotten flavor, as we have become more familiar with the *perceived* aroma—the kind we recognize more from jelly or sweets or even lip balm than from the real thing.

This makes tasting homemade strawberry ice cream all the more special. Sweetness matched with juiciness and a fragrance that travels up the back of your throat and into your nose and memory so pleasingly.

Gariguette are a small, sweet variety of strawberry—the first, eagerly anticipated ones of the year, arriving sometime in late May. The best ones have a funny shape like a rabbit's head and a soft "purple" fruit flavor. They are madly aromatic with an almost synthetic taste similar to that of wild strawberries. Failing these, look for any ripe, sweet-smelling variety that's been grown for flavor rather than supermarket shelf life. I love big red Jubilees, too, although they come a bit later in the season.

Frozen redcurrants or a good tangy redcurrant jelly will improve the texture of this ice cream and give it body—strawberries can tend to be watery, even in peak season.

Try pairing a scoop of this with fresh Pea Pod ice cream (page 74)— really, it works.

500 g/1 lb Gariguette or other in-season strawberries
200 g/¾ cup sugar
25 g/1 oz redcurrants or 1 tablespoon redcurrant jelly (optional)
150 ml/½ cup whole milk
250 ml/1 cup heavy cream
Small pinch of sea salt
4 egg yolks

(recipe continues)

1. To prepare the ice cream: dip the strawberries in cold water to rinse them briefly, and then lay them out on a clean dish towel to drain. Pull or slice away the green crown of leaves, removing the bare minimum of fruit. Slice the berries in half into a clean container.

2. Add half of the sugar and the redcurrants or redcurrant jelly (if using), and stir to combine. Cover the container and leave the fruits to macerate in the fridge overnight.

3. Heat the milk, cream, and salt together in a non-reactive pan, stirring often with a whisk or silicone spatula to prevent it from catching. Once the milk is hot and steaming, whisk the egg yolks and the rest of the sugar together in a separate bowl until combined.

4. Pour the milk in a thin stream over the yolks, whisking continuously. Return all the mix to the pan and cook over low heat until it reaches 82°C/180°F, stirring all the time to avoid curdling the eggs and keeping a close eye on it so as not to let it boil. As soon as your digital thermometer says 82°C/180°F, place the pan in a sink of ice water to cool it down—you can speed up the cooling by stirring it every so often. Once the custard is at room temperature, cover with plastic wrap and chill in the fridge.

5. To make the ice cream: the following day, add the chilled strawberries and any juice to the cold custard and liquidize for a couple of minutes until as smooth as possible. Using a small ladle, push the strawberry custard through a fine-mesh sieve or chinois into a clean container, squeezing hard to extract the maximum smooth custard mix from the seeds.

6. Pour into an ice cream machine and churn until frozen and the texture of whipped cream, 20 to 25 minutes.

7. Scrape the ice cream into a suitable lidded container. Top with a piece of wax paper to limit exposure to air, cover, and freeze until ready to serve. Best eaten within a couple of weeks.

# PRUNE AND EARL GREY

How about this for a simple way to make a sorbet? Succulent *pruneaux d'Agen* are soaked in Earl Grey tea until soft and obliging, with a couple of vivid strips of orange peel to lift the flavor. A week or longer in the fridge not only gives these simple flavors time to harmonize, it also encourages the natural sugars within the fruit to create a saporous syrup. The soaked prunes are then simply pitted, blended, and churned into a sorbet of great delicacy.

This super-easy method of preparation, along with the fruit's natural sweetness, waives any need for additional sugar, making this recipe suitable for diabetics. Try it with heavy cream laced with Armagnac, or with Buffalo Milk, Almond, and Amalfi Lemon (page 27), Novellino Orange Jelly ice cream (page 28), and hot chocolate sauce.

300 g/10 oz Agen prunes (or any other prune you prefer)
Pared zest of ½ orange
2 Earl Grey tea bags
600 ml/2½ cups freshly boiled water (from a kettle)
2 tablespoons sugar (optional, see Note)

(recipe continues)

1. To prepare the sorbet: arrange the prunes in a large cup or deep container, interspacing them with the strips of peel and the tea bags.

2. Measure out the boiled water, add the sugar (if using), and pour this over the prunes. Leave to cool, then cover with plastic wrap and chill in the fridge for a week, turning them every day, or for up to a month.

3. To make the sorbet: pick through the prunes, remove the pits, and discard the strips of zest and tea bags. Liquidize the prunes and all the syrup until perfectly smooth, about 2 minutes.

4. Pour the mix into an ice cream machine and churn according to the machine's instructions. Because the purée is quite thick it should take less time to churn than usual, about 15 minutes.

5. Scrape the sorbet into a suitable lidded container. Top with a piece of wax paper to limit exposure to air, cover, and freeze for an hour before serving.

Note—This sorbet is best eaten within a day or two. If you want to keep it for longer, you could add a couple of tablespoons of sugar to the hot tea mix, stirring to dissolve it before pouring it over the prunes. This will help prevent iciness.

Variation—Dried Blenheim Apricot and Chamomile Tea makes a sunny alternative to this recipe and can be used in just the same quantities. I like using a couple of strips of lemon in place of the orange in this case, too.

# Elderflowers

As familiar to an English summer's day as jam sandwiches and wasps, a good elderflower syrup needs to capture the ephemeral fragrance of the frothy cream-colored flowers. Commercially produced cordial kind of falls flat, and too often the homemade stuff is reminiscent of a cup full of hay fever when it's made badly—and at its worst smells like cats' pee—but there are tips for keeping it bright 'n' breezy.

Pick elderflower heads first thing in the morning—just like the old wives' tales say—when they are like clumps of fresh, white sea foam and free from the buzzing insects and pollution the day brings.

Steep the flowers in cold syrup and leave in a cool place over a few days; that way the flavor isn't "cooked" and you'll have better luck capturing the transient floral sweetness.

Citric acid helps to preserve the syrup and provides the necessary sharp contrast to what is otherwise too flowery.

## Elderflower Syrup

**20 elderflower heads**
**1 kg/5 cups sugar**
**1 kg/5 cups water**
**1 Amalfi or unwaxed lemon**
**1 heaping teaspoon citric acid**

1. First thing in the morning, pick about 20 elderflower heads or fill a big bowl. Back in the kitchen, shake the flower heads free of any dust or insects. Using scissors, snip the sprigs of elderflower blossom into a clean, deep bowl.

2. Bring the sugar and water to a boil in a pan, stirring occasionally to make sure the sugar dissolves. Place the pan in a sink full of ice water to cool. Wash and slice the lemon and add this to the syrup along with the citric acid.

3. Once the syrup is cold, pour it and the lemon slices over the elderflowers, making sure they are fully submerged. Cover the bowl with plastic wrap and chill in the fridge for 4 days.

4. After 4 days, strain the syrup through a fine-mesh sieve or chinois, squeezing the elderflowers to extract as much flavored syrup from them as possible. Bottle and store the syrup in the fridge for up to 2 weeks (or freeze in a suitable container).

# STRAWBERRY AND ELDERFLOWER

The fragrant combination of fresh strawberries and elderflowers is a revelation—flavorful, delicate, and pretty as a posy. The perfect summer dessert.

Whole Amalfi lemon is used to add flavor and pectin to the mix, improving the "body" of the sorbet. Amalfi lemons have softer, milder pith than normal lemons, making it possible to eat them this way.

550 g/1¼ lbs strawberries
300 ml/1¼ cups elderflower syrup (see opposite)
½ Amalfi lemon (or use ½ unwaxed lemon), chopped

1. To prepare the sorbet: rinse the strawberries and then lay them out on a clean dish towel to drain. Cut away the leaves, removing the bare minimum of fruit. Slice the berries in half into a clean container.

2. Add the elderflower syrup and the chopped lemon—juice and seeds and all—and liquidize together until perfectly smooth, 2 to 3 minutes. Using a small ladle, pass the purée through a fine-mesh sieve or chinois. Squeeze hard to extract as much purée as possible, then discard the strawberry seeds and fibers. Chill the mix in the fridge for a couple of hours until completely cold.

3. To make the sorbet: pour the strawberry purée into an ice cream machine and churn according to the machine's instructions until frozen and creamy-looking, 20 to 25 minutes.

4. Transfer the sorbet to a suitable lidded container. Top with a piece of wax paper to limit exposure to air, cover, and freeze until ready to serve. Best eaten within 2 weeks.

Variation—Make a basic simple syrup with 190 g/1 cup sugar and 190 ml/¾ cup water, then use in place of the elderflower syrup to make an excellent Strawberry and Amalfi Lemon sorbet.

# CUCUMBER AND SOUR CREAM

Novelty ice creams are fun to try the first time, but unless you want to lick the bowl clean they don't get added to my list of favorites. Nobody needs to have uneaten ice cream languishing in the freezer getting fish finger-y and frosty. Freezer space is important—you need some room for peas and ice cubes too!

I promise, though, that this recipe is no fad. It's the most refreshing and pacifying of all ice cream flavors—what could be cooler? It has become a summer tradition, looked forward to—and not just by me.

Salting the cucumber first draws out excess water, concentrates the flavor, and improves the texture of the ice cream. The salt should be barely discernable in the end result, though. Incredible combined with Strawberry Salad (page 106) and Dill Seed ice cream (page 35) or on its own on a really sweaty day.

1 medium cucumber (about 250 g/8 oz), homegrown or from a farmers' market, if possible (less watery)
1 teaspoon coarse sea salt
325 ml/1¼ cups whole milk
2 whole eggs
150 g/¾ cup sugar
300 ml/1¼ cups sour cream

1. To prepare the ice cream: first peel your cucumber—use a vegetable peeler to remove all the tough green skin. Cut the cucumber in half lengthwise and use a teaspoon to scrape out and discard the watery seeds. Dice the cucumber halves, then toss them in a bowl with the sea salt. Tip them into a colander in the sink to drip. After 20 minutes, rinse them briefly in a bowl of cold water and set on a clean dish towel to drain. Chill in the fridge in a lidded container overnight.

(recipe continues)

2. Heat the milk in a non-reactive pan. Stir often, using a whisk or silicone spatula, to prevent it from catching. Once the milk is steaming, whisk the whole eggs and sugar together in a separate bowl until combined.

3. Pour the hot milk over the eggs in a thin stream, whisking continuously. Return all the mix to the pan and cook over low heat until it reaches 82°C/180°F, stirring all the time to avoid curdling the eggs, and keeping a close eye on it so as not to let it boil. As soon as your digital thermometer says 82°C/180°F, place the pan in a sink of ice water to cool. Add the sour cream to the custard and whisk it in—you can speed up the cooling process by stirring the mix every so often. Once the custard is at room temperature, scrape it in a clean container, cover with plastic wrap, and chill in the fridge.

4. To make the ice cream: the following day the cucumber will have expelled more water; pour this away, then blitz the cucumber and custard together in a blender. Blitz for 2 to 3 minutes until very, very smooth—you don't want any frozen lumps of cucumber in this ice cream. Use a small ladle to push the cucumber custard through a fine-mesh sieve or chinois into a clean container.

5. Pour the custard into an ice cream machine and churn according to the machine's instructions until frozen and the texture of stiff whipped cream, usually 20 to 25 minutes.

6. Scrape the ice cream into a suitable lidded container. Top with a piece of wax paper to limit exposure to air, cover, and freeze until ready to serve. Best eaten within a week.

# MINT CHIP

This is one of the first recipes for which I got to flex my ice cream muscles—testing it out at St. John Bread & Wine, where we served it with hot chocolate sauce. It's a simple milk ice, thickened with tapioca or cornstarch (egg interferes with the fresh mint flavor, making it taste a bit too much like dinner), then briefly steeped with masses of fresh mint leaves.

Each time anyone ordered it at St. John, I'd send it out then peep over the counter to watch as they took the first taste—never getting bored of their surprised and happy reactions.

I've included the option of adding lightly toasted slivered almonds in this recipe—a very good suggestion my photographer Grant made when we were shooting the pictures for this book. They provide an irresistible crunchiness.

130 g/²⁄₃ cup sugar
15 g/1 tablespoon tapioca starch or cornstarch
500 ml/1¾ cups whole milk
150 ml/¾ cup heavy cream
20 g/¾ oz fresh mint leaves, rinsed and picked
50 g/1¾ oz dark chocolate, grated
20 g/¾ oz toasted blanched slivered almonds (optional)

1. To prepare the milk ice: in a bowl, whisk 2 tablespoons of the sugar into the tapioca starch or cornstarch.

2. Heat the milk and cream with the remaining sugar, stirring often, using a whisk or silicone spatula, to prevent it from catching. Once the liquid is hot and steaming, pour it into the bowl containing the starch. Whisk constantly to combine it well without lumps forming.

(recipe continues)

3. Return all the mix to the pan and cook over low heat, whisking constantly, just until it starts to simmer. Remove the pan from the heat, stir in the mint leaves, then cover the pan tightly with plastic wrap and place it in a sink full of ice water to cool.

4. After 15 minutes, taste the thickened milk; if the flavor of mint is lively and pronounced, pass the mixture through a fine-mesh sieve or chinois, squeezing the leaves to extract as much flavor as possible. Otherwise, leave the mix to cool completely, another 10 to 15 minutes, before straining and discarding the leaves. Return the pan to the sink to cool completely before covering and chilling overnight in the fridge.

5. To make the milk ice: the following day liquidize the mix with an immersion blender for 1 minute to emulsify completely; this will also help liquefy the mix.

6. Pour the mix into an ice cream machine and churn according to the machine's instructions until frozen and the texture of whipped cream, usually 20 to 25 minutes.

7. Scrape the milk ice into a suitable lidded container, sprinkling with gratings of dark chocolate and slivers of almond as you go. Top with a piece of wax paper to limit exposure to air, cover, and freeze until ready to serve.

Note—This ice is best eaten within a week: the recipe contains no egg yolk and little cream, so it freezes hard and can become icy otherwise.

# SWISS VANILLA

When I teach my class at The School of Artisan Food up in Nottinghamshire, we make up to a dozen different vanilla ice creams in a day—gelato, egg-free, no-cook, parfaits, "super premium," raw milk, and aged recipes, to name a few. The idea is to gain an understanding of how various different methods and ingredients can affect the texture and flavor of ice cream.

It's been interesting to note that in eight years of teaching this class, this simple vanilla ice cream recipe consistently wins the popular vote at the 5 p.m. tasting. It's not the richest and it doesn't use any complicated ingredients, but it has the fresh, creamy, smooth texture that everyone looks for in an ice cream, and is not too sweet.

It's so called because I always liked the film *Who's That Girl*, especially the bit where Madonna is asked: "What school did you go to—was it Swiss?" And she answers: "Yeah, the Swissest." Since having my trusty Swiss ice cream machines, which—more than any other piece of equipment I've bought—have never let me down, Swiss has become a synonym for best.

1 vanilla pod
300 ml/1¼ cups whole milk
300 ml/1¼ cups heavy cream
Pinch of sea salt
3 large egg yolks
110 g/½ cup sugar

1. To prepare the ice cream: split the vanilla pod using the tip of a sharp knife, scrape out the seeds, and place both seeds and pod in a non-reactive pan with the milk, cream, and sea salt. Stir often, using a whisk or silicone spatula, to prevent it from catching. Once the liquid is hot and steaming, whisk the egg yolks and sugar together in a separate bowl until combined.

2. Pour the hot liquid over the yolks in a thin stream, whisking continuously. Return all the mix to the pan and cook over low heat until it reaches 82°C/180°F, stirring all the time to avoid curdling the eggs and keeping a close eye on it so as not to let it boil. As soon as your digital thermometer says 82°C/180°F, place the pan in a sink of ice water to cool. Speed up the cooling process by stirring the mix every so often. Once the custard is at room temperature, transfer it into a clean container, cover with plastic wrap, and chill.

3. To make the ice cream: the following day, use a small ladle to push the custard through a fine-mesh sieve or chinois into a clean container. Save the vanilla pod (you can rinse and dry it, then use it for vanilla sugar or homemade vanilla extract; see page 19), then liquidize the cold custard with an immersion blender for a minute to emulsify.

4. Pour the custard into an ice cream machine and churn according to the machine's instructions until frozen and the texture of whipped cream, 20 to 25 minutes.

5. Transfer the ice cream to a suitable lidded container. Top with a piece of wax paper to limit exposure to air, cover, and freeze until ready to serve.

Note—This recipe really does benefit from being "aged" (see page 20) in the fridge overnight before churning. The texture will thicken and have better mouthfeel, and you get a warm long-lasting flavor from the vanilla pod.

# APRICOT NOYAU

A few years ago, late at night in bed and high on Italian eBay, I bought several thousand pounds worth of 1960s Italian ice cream machinery from a used catering-equipment salesman in northern Italy. I hired a van and undertook an insane 24-hour drive to Turin and back to bring the 2-ton machines to the UK. Once home, they sat, unfixable, in storage for approximately six years, quietly leaking thick black oil and defunct coolant over my garage floor until I sold them for scrap metal last summer.

The upside to this story was that en route home we stopped at a market in Lyon where I took advantage of every bit of negative space in the van and bought a stall's entire stock of very ripe apricots to bring back with me. It made enough ice cream for that whole summer and it was extraordinarily good—the delicious but slightly poisonous marzipan flavor of the "noyau" or kernels acting as a bitter reminder against late-night eBay purchases.

About 375 g/13 oz fresh apricots
150 g/¾ cup sugar
150 ml/½ cup whole milk
200 ml/1 cup heavy cream
3 egg yolks
1 teaspoon honey (optional)

1. To prepare the ice cream: slice the apricots in half and remove the pits; keep these to one side. Cook the apricot halves very lightly just until the fruit collapses. If using a microwave, place the fruit in a heatproof bowl with a tablespoon of water. Cover the bowl with plastic wrap and cook on high until tender, 2 to 3 minutes. Otherwise simmer the apricot halves gently in a non-reactive pan, just until they are cooked through and piping hot (do not boil). Cool in a sink of ice water, then cover and chill in the fridge.

(recipe continues)

2. Place a clean dish towel on a hard surface, then line the apricot pits up along the middle of the towel. Fold the dish towel in half over the apricot pits to cover them, and then firmly crack each pit with a rolling pin (the dish towel prevents bits of the shell from flying all over the kitchen). Try to hit hard enough to crack the shell, but not so energetically that you completely obliterate it—you want to be able to rescue the kernels from inside the shell afterward.

3. Pick the tiny kernel from each shell, then grind them in a mortar and pestle or spice grinder with 20 g/2 tablespoons of the sugar.

4. Heat the milk, cream, and the ground kernel mix in a pan, stirring often with a whisk or silicone spatula to prevent it from catching. As soon as the milk is hot and steaming, whisk the yolks with the remaining sugar and honey (if using) until combined.

5. Pour the hot liquid over the yolk mix in a thin stream, whisking constantly as you do so, then return all the mix to the pan. Cook gently over low heat, stirring all the time, until the mix reaches 82°C/180°F. As soon as your digital thermometer says 82°C/180°F, remove the pan from the heat and set it in a sink full of ice water to cool—you can speed up the process by stirring it every so often. Once entirely cold, pour the custard into a clean container, cover, and chill in the fridge.

6. To make the ice cream: the following day, use a spatula to scrape the chilled apricots into the custard, then blend together with an immersion blender until very smooth—blitz until there are only small flecks of apricot skin visible in the mix, at least 2 minutes. Using a small ladle, push the apricot custard through a fine-mesh sieve or chinois into a clean container, squeezing hard to extract as much smooth custard mix as possible. Discard the bits of skin and kernel.

7. Pour the custard into an ice cream machine and churn according to the machine's instructions until frozen and the texture of whipped cream, usually 20 to 25 minutes.

8. Transfer the ice cream to a suitable lidded container. Top with a piece of wax paper to limit exposure to air, cover, and freeze until ready to serve.

# My Favorite Flavor

If I get asked what my favorite ice cream is—which happens quite often—the first thing I do is panic: my favorite … this week? Then I remember peach ice cream …

You rarely see peach ice cream offered as a scoop unless you happen to live in one of those peach tree–blessed states like California, South Carolina, or Georgia. Even when you do, it's usually a plain white ice cream with frozen chunks of peach studded through, which leaves me feeling cheated. This is not my idea of peach ice cream.

I always remember being struck reading Roald Dahl's *James and the Giant Peach* at the bit when James crawls through a juicy peach tunnel to his new peach pit home, eating handfuls of sweet yellow peach flesh as he goes. This is what eating peach ice cream should be like—an all encompassing flavor that surrounds you— flavor that you can smell! Surround yourself with peach ice cream!

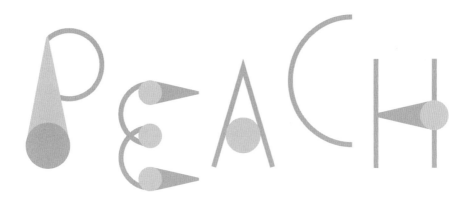

This recipe makes rich silky custard the color of your great-aunt's bathroom suite, with the unparalleled flavor and breathy fragrance of fresh peaches. Best inhaled when it is freshly made, or at least within one week, as the flavor is soon lost.

Serve with Yellow Peach and Basil sorbet (page 128) or Wild Blueberry ice cream (page 108).

4 large ripe peaches (about 650 g/1½ lb)
Zest and juice of 1 lemon, preferably unwaxed
210 g/1 cup sugar
160 ml/¾ cup whole milk
300 ml/1¼ cups heavy cream
Pinch of sea salt
4 egg yolks

1. To prepare the ice cream: prepare the peaches by rinsing and then halving them, collecting any juice in a bowl. Remove the pits, quarter, and roughly chop the fruit into the bowl. Add the zest and the juice of the lemon and 50 g/¼ cup of the sugar, stir gently, cover with plastic wrap, and leave to macerate in the fridge.

2. Bring the milk and cream, plus a pinch of sea salt, to a simmer in a non-reactive pan. Stir often, using a whisk or silicone spatula, to prevent it from catching. Once the liquid is hot and steaming, whisk the egg yolks and the rest of the sugar together in a separate bowl until combined.

3. Pour the hot liquid over the yolks in a thin stream, whisking continuously. Return all the mix to the pan and cook over low heat until it reaches 82°C/180°F. Stir constantly to avoid curdling the eggs, and

(recipe continues)

keep a close eye on it so as not to let it boil. As soon as your digital thermometer says 82°C/180°F, place the pan in a sink of ice water to cool—you can speed up the cooling process by stirring the mix every so often. Once the custard is at room temperature, transfer it into a clean container, cover with plastic wrap, and chill.

4. To make the ice cream: the following day, use a spatula to scrape the chilled peaches into the custard, then blend the two together with an immersion blender until very smooth—blitz until there are only small flecks of peach skin visible in the mix, at least 2 minutes. Using a small ladle, push the peach custard through a fine-mesh sieve or chinois into a clean container, squeezing hard to extract as much smooth custard mix as possible. Discard the peach skin.

5. Pour the custard into an ice cream machine and churn according to the machine's instructions, usually 20 to 25 minutes, or until frozen and the texture of whipped cream.

6. Scrape the ice cream into a suitable lidded container. Top with a piece of wax paper to limit exposure to air, cover, and freeze until ready to serve. Best consumed when it's freshly made, or at least within a week, as the flavor is soon lost.

Note—Macerating the peaches, skin on, with sugar and lemon overnight draws the sharp sweet flavor from the fruit, and the color and aroma from the skin (which later gets strained out), giving the ice cream a faintly pink tint and extra perfume.

# TOMATO AND WHITE PEACH

One of the greatest pleasures I know is to eat along with the characters from books and on TV shows. I spent hours reading Laura Ingalls Wilder's *Farmer Boy* when I was growing up, stomach rumbling in thrall to her mouth-watering descriptions of frontier foods.

I'm pretty sure that I could recite the chapter off by heart where Almanzo Wilder makes ice cream in a tin pail using sawdust, ice, and salt—I've tasted it in my imagination a million times. In another *Little House* book there's a passage I always found incredible: on a hot day Laura's ma slices up a ripe tomato, then serves it covered with cream and sugar—to be eaten like a peach!

I mulled over the idea of a tomato ice cream for years (tomatoes *are* actually fruits, so it ought to make sense) before finally getting a chance to test it out using a real old-fashioned hand-cranked machine on a ranch I was teaching at in Colorado. Hand-cranked ice cream machines are fun and although the tomato ice cream looked delicious—creamy and candy-pink—no one could swallow the stuff; it was just too weird.

(recipe continues)

I put the difference in taste down to the fact that Laura Ingalls and family were too far from peaches, and had come close to starving in previous years because of drought and crop failure. And we were very far from starving. Also, I suppose tastes change.

Instead, I've settled upon this simple and refreshing recipe, unusual rather than flat-out weird, and very lovely. It produces an elegant, shell-pink sorbet with soft sweetness from the tomato and fruitiness from the white peach.

130 g/⅔ cup sugar
130 ml/⅔ cup water
3 white peaches or 4 flat white peaches
2 ripe tomatoes (San Marzano are particularly flavorful)

1. To prepare the sorbet: heat the sugar and water together in a pan to make a simple syrup, stirring to dissolve the grains of sugar. As soon as the syrup starts to simmer, remove it from the heat. Set aside to cool and then chill in the fridge until needed.

2. Rinse the tomatoes and peaches, slice them into a bowl, cover with the cool simple syrup, and chill in the fridge for at least 4 hours, giving it time to really draw the flavor out of the tomato and peach skins.

3. Remove the macerated fruits from the fridge and blend them for 2 minutes until very smooth. Pass the mixture through a fine-mesh sieve or chinois, discarding the skin and seeds.

4. To make the sorbet: pour the shell-pink purée into an ice cream machine and churn according to the machine's instructions, usually 20 to 25 minutes, or until frozen and thick and creamy-looking.

5. Transfer the sorbet to a suitable lidded container. Top with a piece of wax paper to limit exposure to air, cover, and freeze until ready to serve. Eat within a fortnight.

# NECTARINE AND TARRAGON

Here's a little secret: despite having claimed in these pages that peach is the best ice cream flavor, in fact nectarines are my very favorite drupes to scoop. (Yes! Drupes! This is a real botanical name given to this group of stone fruits and the reason, if someone tells you that you have a drupey arse, you should be really pleased.) Peaches have a more subtle perfume, but nectarines just pip them with their rich, tart flesh. They make velvety, sumptuous ice cream with well-balanced flavor.

The soft note of sweet anise-flavored tarragon really complements the ice cream—especially if you use white nectarines.

500 g/1 lb ripe nectarines (3 to 4 fruits)
Zest and juice of 1 lemon, preferably unwaxed
190 g/1 cup sugar
100 ml/½ cup whole milk
300 ml/1 cup heavy cream
3 egg yolks
30 g/1 oz fresh tarragon

1. To prepare the ice cream: rinse the nectarines and halve them, collecting any juice in a bowl. Slice the flesh in chunks from around the pit and drop it into the bowl. Add the lemon zest and juice and 50 g/¼ cup of the sugar. Mix this together gently, cover the bowl with plastic wrap, and leave to macerate in the fridge overnight.

2. Bring the milk and cream to a simmer in a non-reactive pan, stirring often with a whisk or silicone spatula to prevent it from catching. Once the liquid is hot and steaming, whisk the egg yolks and the remaining sugar together in a separate bowl until combined.

3. Pour the hot milk over the yolks in a thin stream, whisking continuously. Return all the mix to the pan and cook over low heat until it reaches 82°C/180°F. Stir constantly to avoid curdling the eggs and keep a close eye on it so as not to let it boil. As soon as your digital thermometer says 82°C/180°F, remove the pan from the heat, add the tarragon leaves, and stir to submerge them in the custard. Cover the pan with plastic wrap, then place in a sink full of ice water to cool for 30 minutes. Once the custard is at room temperature, use a spatula to scrape it through a fine-mesh sieve or chinois. Squeeze hard on the tarragon to extract as much flavor as possible. Discard the leaves, cover the container with plastic wrap, and chill in the fridge.

4. To make the ice cream: the following day, use a spatula to scrape the chilled nectarines and all their lemony juices into the tarragon custard, then blitz until as smooth as possible, 2 to 3 minutes, or until there are only small flecks of red nectarine skin visible in the mix. Using a small ladle, push the custard through a fine-mesh sieve or chinois into a clean container, squeezing hard to extract as much smooth custard mix as possible. Discard the bits of nectarine skin.

5. Pour the custard into an ice cream machine and churn according to the machine's instructions until frozen and the texture of whipped cream, 20 to 25 minutes.

6. Scrape the ice cream into a suitable lidded container. Top with a piece of wax paper to limit exposure to air, cover, and freeze until ready to serve. Best eaten within a fortnight.

Variation—White peaches will work just as well as nectarines in this recipe.

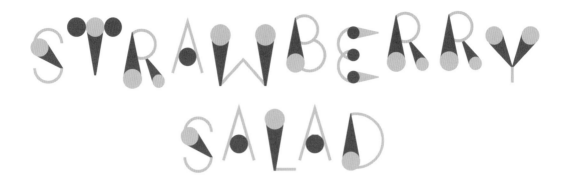

# STRAWBERRY SALAD

This Schiaparelli-pink ice cream "salad" is made from a blend of fresh strawberries, Amalfi lemons, and unwaxed oranges—all used whole. Don't be put off by using every bit of the citrus; the unpalatable bits of seed and pith get sieved away eventually. For best results seek out Amalfi lemons for their thick, mild pith or, failing that, use unwaxed lemons and oranges.

Macerating the berries and citrus together, then whizzing them up smoothly into the custard, is a device to add pectin and just the right amount of acidity to the ice cream base. The results are a full-bodied, elastic-textured ice cream, with tangy multi-dimensional strawberry flavor. Ultra strawberry, in other words.

I learned not to be afraid of using whole citrus after a winter spent working in a pastry shop in Sicily with a sprightly couple of octogenarians who came in to help make marmalades. They ate chunks of raw Amalfi lemon throughout the day, and extolled the virtues of its mild pith and sweet flesh with such twinkle (and such white teeth) I couldn't help but be curious to try it myself.

Oddly, after all this careful blending and sieving, the results taste very much like strawberry Starburst candy—but that's okay because the pink ones were always the best. Made to make your mouth water.

400 g/1 lb strawberries
Half a lemon (preferably Amalfi lemon)
Half an unwaxed orange
190 g/1 cup sugar
150 ml/¾ cup whole milk
250 ml/1 cup heavy cream
Tiny pinch of sea salt
5 egg yolks

1. To prepare the ice cream: dip the strawberries into a sink or bowlful of cold water to rinse them, and then lay them out on a clean dish towel to drai:.. Pull or slice away the green crown of leaves, removing the bare minimum of fruit. Slice the berries in half into a clean bowl.

2. Chop the citrus fruit (peel, pith, seeds, and all) into small chunks and weigh out a 90 g/3-oz mix of lemon and orange. Add this, along with any spilled juice, to the strawberries. Add half the sugar and stir gently to combine. Cover the bowl and leave to macerate in the fridge overnight.

3. Heat the milk, cream, and salt together in a non-reactive pan. Stir often, using a whisk or silicone spatula, to prevent it from catching. Once the milk is hot and steaming, whisk the egg yolks and remaining sugar together in a separate bowl until combined.

4. Pour the hot milk in a thin stream over the yolks, whisking continuously. Return all the mix to the pan and cook over low heat until it reaches 82°C/180°F, stirring all the time to avoid curdling the eggs and keeping a close eye on it so as not to let it boil. As soon as your digital thermometer says 82°C/180°F, place the pan in a sink of ice water to cool it down—you can speed up the cooling process by stirring it every so often. Once the custard is at room temperature, cover with plastic wrap and chill in the fridge.

5. To make the ice cream: the following day, add the chilled strawberry salad and any juice to the cold custard and blitz together with a blender until very smooth, at least 3 minutes. Using a small ladle, push the strawberry custard through a fine-mesh sieve or chinois into a clean container, squeezing hard to extract as much smooth custard mix as possible.

6. Pour into an ice cream machine and churn according to the machine's instructions until frozen and the texture of whipped cream, usually 20 to 25 minutes.

7. Transfer the ice cream into a suitable lidded container. Top with a piece of wax paper to limit exposure to air, cover, and freeze until ready to serve.

# WILD BLUEBERRY

This is how the sky-blue Italian ice cream flavor *Puffo* (or "Smurf") ought to taste—but doesn't. Embarrassingly, my fallback word to define the flavor of this ice cream is simply "blue." This suggests a lack of imagination—using the word "minerality" would be more elegant. My excuse is that the taste of blueberries is hard to characterize, given that much of the satisfaction gained from eating them comes from their firm, popping texture. So if possible, use wild blueberries (also known as bilberries or huckleberries), as they have infinitely more indefinable flavor than cultivated varieties.

300 g/10 oz blueberries
130 ml/¾ cup whole milk
350 ml/1¼ cups heavy cream
4 egg yolks
140 g/¾ cup sugar

1. To prepare the ice cream: cook the blueberries very lightly. If using a microwave, place them in a heatproof bowl along with a tablespoon of water, cover the bowl with plastic wrap, and cook for 2 to 3 minutes on high. Otherwise simmer them gently in a non-reactive pan with a drop of water just until they are tender, bursting and piping hot (do not boil). Cool in a sink of ice water; once cold, cover and chill in the fridge.

2. Heat the milk and cream together in a pan over low heat, stirring every so often with a whisk or silicone spatula. When the liquid reaches a simmer, whisk the egg yolks and the sugar together in a separate bowl until combined.

3. Pour the hot liquid over the yolks in a thin stream, whisking continuously. Return all the mix to the pan and cook over low heat until it reaches 82°C/180°F. Stir constantly to avoid curdling the eggs, and keep a close eye so as not to let it boil. As soon as your digital thermometer says 82°C/180°F, place the pan in a sink of ice water to cool. Speed up the cooling process by stirring the mix every so often. Once the custard is at room temperature, transfer it into a clean container, cover with plastic wrap, and chill in the fridge.

4. To make the ice cream: the following day, use a spatula to scrape the chilled blueberries and their juice into the custard. Liquidize with a blender or immersion blender until very smooth, about 2 minutes— the mix will thicken considerably as though set with gelatin. Use a small ladle to push the thick custard through a fine-mesh sieve or chinois into a clean container. Discard any seeds and the fruit skin.

5. Pour the slate-blue custard into an ice cream machine and churn according to the machine's instructions until frozen and the texture of whipped cream, 20 to 25 minutes.

6. Scrape the ice cream into a suitable lidded container. Top with a piece of wax paper to limit exposure to air, cover, and freeze until ready to serve.

Note—As well as being packed full of vitamins, blueberries are high in natural pectin, which has an amazing gelling effect on an ice cream custard; you will notice that it thickens this recipe almost to the point of setting it.

You can use this tip and try adding a few blueberries to more watery fruit ice creams and sorbet bases to help their texture considerably without affecting the flavor much.

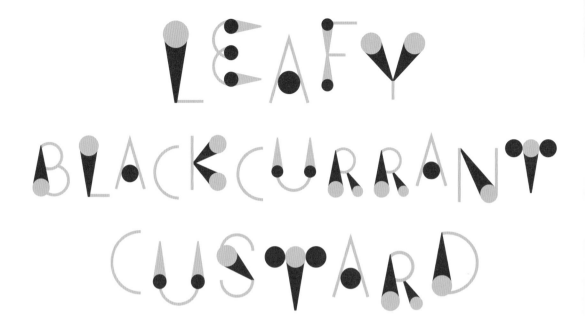

# LEAFY BLACKCURRANT CUSTARD

One of my earliest smell memories is being on a farm in Devon picking blackcurrants, at about age 3, standing on the red earth and swishing the leaves, releasing fumes of their intoxicating white acid drop fragrance—so odd and so different from the taste of the fresh currants. It's good—like the way sweet, fruity tomatoes and the green smell of their stalks magnify each other's best qualities. If only somebody would make a perfume of this and stop me having to slather blackcurrant leaf ice cream behind my ears every day.

If you are lucky enough to grow blackcurrants, adding a few leaves to the custard base of this recipe elevates it to a different level. In any case, the flavor of this ice cream is supernatural. The low water content and high amount of pectin in the currants contribute to a very well–behaved ice cream: rich, smooth, and custardy but tangy, too, and deep magenta pink.

150 ml/¾ cup whole milk
350 ml/1¼ cups heavy cream
Pinch of sea salt
5 to 6 large fresh blackcurrant leaves, washed (optional)
280 g/9 oz blackcurrants
3 egg yolks
160 g/¾ cup sugar

(recipe continues)

1. To prepare the ice cream: heat the milk, cream, and salt together. As soon as the liquid reaches a simmer, stir in the blackcurrant leaves to submerge. Remove from the heat, cover the pan with plastic wrap, and leave to infuse for 30 minutes in a sink of ice water.

2. Meanwhile, rinse the blackcurrants and pick them from their stalks. The best way to cook them is very lightly in a microwave: add 2 tablespoons of water, cover the bowl with plastic wrap, and zap them for a couple of minutes. Otherwise simmer them very gently in a non-reactive pan just until they are tender and bursting (do not boil). Cool the bowl in a sink of ice water, and once the berries are cold, cover and chill in the fridge.

3. Strain the now-fragrant milk and cream mixture into a clean non-reactive pan and bring to a simmer. Stir often, using a whisk or silicone spatula, to prevent it from catching. Once the liquid is steaming, whisk the egg yolks and the sugar together in a separate bowl until combined.

4. Pour the hot liquid over the yolks in a thin stream, whisking continuously. Return all the mix to the pan and cook over low heat until it reaches 82°C/180°F. Stir constantly to avoid curdling the eggs and keep a close eye on it so as not to let it boil. As soon as your digital thermometer says 82°C/180°F, place the pan in a sink of ice water to cool. Speed up the cooling process by stirring the mix every so often. Once the custard is at room temperature, scrape it into a clean container, cover with plastic wrap, and chill in the fridge.

5. To make the ice cream: the following day, use a spatula to scrape the chilled blackcurrants into the custard then liquidize the two parts together with an immersion blender until the mixture turns a gorgeous purple color and is very smooth, 2 to 3 minutes. Using a small ladle, push the blackcurrant custard through a fine-mesh sieve or chinois into a clean container to remove the seeds.

6. Pour into an ice cream machine and churn according to the machine's instructions until frozen and the texture of whipped cream, 20 to 25 minutes.

7. Scrape the ice cream into a suitable lidded container. Top with a piece of wax paper to limit exposure to air, cover, and freeze until ready to serve.

# LOGAN BERRY

There's a short window of about a fortnight every July when the heavily scented loganberry—the most dreamy flavoring for ice cream imaginable—comes into season. (The berries don't smell, or even taste very strongly raw—the magic happens once they're cooked.) But, like mulberries, they are too fragile and juicy to supply commercially, and they can prove notoriously difficult to find.

At this point, every pastry chef, jam maker, and cake baker in London with a clue goes quiet—they are just itching for a day off so they can zoom down the motorway to Kent or Essex for a morning fruit-picking—and they keep their cards close to their chest until their haul is safely back in the kitchen. Only at this point do they finally hit Instagram for all they're worth.

If you know a farm that cultivates these jewels, be careful who you tell about it, and pick as fast as you can when you get the chance. Even if this means you make gallons of loganberry ice cream and eat it for months to come, you won't have any regrets!

If you can't get hold of loganberries, then other berries will work well too (see Variations, page 115).

(recipe continues)

320 g/10 oz loganberries
100 ml/½ cup whole milk
300 ml/1 cup heavy cream
4 egg yolks
130 g/⅔ cup sugar

1. To prepare the ice cream: cook the loganberries very gently. If using a microwave, place them in a heatproof bowl with 2 tablespoons of water, cover the bowl with plastic wrap, and cook for 2 to 3 minutes on high. Otherwise, simmer them gently in a lidded non-reactive pan just until they are tender, bursting, and piping hot. Do not boil. Cool in a sink of ice water. Once cold, cover and chill in the fridge.

2. Heat the milk and cream together, stirring every so often with a whisk or silicone spatula. When the liquid reaches a simmer, whisk the egg yolks and sugar together in a separate bowl until combined.

3. Pour the hot liquid over the yolks in a thin stream, whisking continuously. Return all the mix to the pan and cook over low heat until it reaches 82°C/180°F. Stir constantly to avoid curdling the eggs and keep a close eye on it so as not to let it boil. As soon as your digital thermometer says 82°C/180°F, place the pan in a sink of ice water to cool—you can speed up the cooling process by stirring the mix every so often. Once the custard is at room temperature, scrape it into a clean container, cover with plastic wrap, and chill in the fridge.

4. To make the ice cream: the following day, use a spatula to scrape the chilled loganberries into the custard, then liquidize the mixture with an immersion blender until it turns a deep pink and is very smooth, 2 to 3 minutes. Use a small ladle to push the custard through a fine-mesh sieve or chinois to remove all the seeds.

5. Pour the custard into an ice cream machine and churn according to the machine's instructions until frozen and the texture of whipped cream, usually 20 to 25 minutes.

6. Scrape the ice cream into a suitable lidded container. Top with a piece of wax paper, cover, and freeze until ready to serve.

Variations—You can make blackberry, raspberry, or tayberry (a cross between a blackberry and a raspberry) ice cream using the same quantity as in the recipe.

# The Lemon Verbena Bush

In a park in Elephant and Castle, behind a very basic concession stand that sells tea from a vending machine, grows a lemon verbena bush the size of a minivan. Throughout winter it's a skeleton of spindly sticks, then in midspring a green neon mist descends upon it, and it comes to life. By summertime, every year without fail, it is flush with slender lemon-scented leaves. You only need to run a hand along the length of a branch—the leaves are rough and sandy like little cats' tongues— to release its compelling, oily fragrance.

Nobody pays it any attention as they drink their tea, and I can pick a plastic bagful every now and again without making the slightest impression on the plant. The leaves dry well and can be refreshed in hot water to make a delicious tisane, magically turning bright green as though come to life again. Otherwise they are easy to infuse in ice creams and custards.

# LEMON VERBENA

I like this one with Leafy Blackcurrant Custard (page 110) and Kumquat Custard (page 31) or rippled with Citrus Gel (page 223).

300 ml/1¼ cups whole milk
300 ml/1¼ cups heavy cream
3 egg yolks
125 g/½ cup plus 2 tablespoons sugar
50 g/2 oz lemon verbena leaves (ideally fresh, but if not, dried)

1. To prepare the ice cream: heat the milk and cream in a non-reactive pan, stirring often to prevent it from catching. Once the mixture is steaming, whisk together the egg yolks and sugar in a separate bowl.

2. Pour the hot milk and cream over the yolks in a thin stream, whisking continuously. Return all the mix to the pan and cook over low heat until it reaches 82°C/180°F, stirring all the time to avoid curdling, and making sure it doesn't boil. As soon as your digital thermometer says 82°C/180°F, remove the pan from the heat, add the lemon verbena leaves, and blitz with an immersion blender until the custard turns pale green, 2 to 3 minutes.

3. Pass the mixture into a bowl through a fine-mesh sieve or chinois, squeezing the blitzed leaves with the back of a small ladle to extract as much flavor as possible. Discard the leaves. Cool the bowl of verbena custard in a sink of ice water, then cover and refrigerate overnight.

4. To make the ice cream: the following day, blitz the custard for 1 minute using an immersion blender. Pour the custard into an ice cream machine and churn according to the machine's instructions until frozen and the texture of whipped cream, 20 to 25 minutes.

5. Scrape the ice cream into a suitable lidded container. Top with a piece of wax paper, cover, and freeze until ready to serve.

# GREEN GOOSEBERRY FOOL

Who could resist vitamin-y, prickly green gooseberry and chiffony egg custard, folded with puffs of crisp meringue? Only a fool!

*For the meringue*
1 egg white
Pinch of sea salt
Superfine sugar (you'll need double the weight of the egg white)

*For the ice cream*
400 g/1 lb green gooseberries
110 ml/½ cup whole milk
250 ml/1 cup heavy cream
2 extra-large egg yolks
150 g/¾ cup sugar

1. To make the meringue: preheat the oven to about 300°F and line a baking sheet with parchment.

2. Weigh the egg white into a large, spotlessly clean and dry mixing bowl. It will weigh around 30 g/1 oz. Add the salt and whisk together until very stiff and dry looking. This will take 6 to 8 minutes if done properly, so using a hand-held electric whisk is a good idea.

3. Measure out double the weight of the egg white in superfine sugar (about 60 g/2 oz). Add the sugar to the beaten egg white little by little, sprinkling in spoonfuls at a time all the while continuing to whisk. Once all of the sugar has been incorporated, continue to whisk

the mix for about 10 minutes until the sugar has completely dissolved and the meringue is glossy, thick, and voluminous.

4. Scrape the meringue out onto the lined baking sheet, smooth into a bird's nest shape, and bake for 1 hour 25 minutes, or until very pale gold and crisp. Leave to cool in the turned-off oven. Once cold, store in a dry, airtight container.

5. To prepare the ice cream: rinse the gooseberries. Don't worry about trimming the flower and stem ends; they will be sieved away later. The best way to cook the gooseberries is very lightly in a microwave: add 2 tablespoons of water, cover the bowl with plastic wrap, and cook for 2 to 3 minutes on high. Otherwise, simmer them gently in a non-reactive pan just until they are tender and bursting and look milky and opaque (do not boil). Cool them in the pan in a sink of ice water. Once cool, cover and chill the gooseberries in the fridge.

6. Heat the milk and cream together, stirring every so often. When the liquid reaches a simmer, whisk the egg yolks and the sugar together in a separate bowl until combined.

7. Pour the hot liquid over the yolks in a thin stream, whisking continuously. Return all the mix to the pan and cook over low heat until it reaches 82°C/180°F. Stir constantly to avoid curdling, and make sure it doesn't boil. As soon as your digital thermometer says 82°C/180°F, place the pan in a sink of ice water to cool, stirring the mix occasionally. Once the custard is at room temperature, scrape it into a clean container, cover with plastic wrap, and chill in the fridge.

8. To make the ice cream: the following day, add the chilled gooseberries and any juice to the cold custard and liquidize for a couple of minutes until smooth and pale green. Using a small ladle, push the custard through a fine-mesh sieve or chinois into a clean container, squeezing hard to extract the maximum custard mix from the seeds.

9. Pour the custard into an ice cream machine and churn according to the machine's instructions until frozen and the texture of whipped cream, usually 20 to 25 minutes.

10. Scrape the ice cream into a suitable lidded container. Working quickly, sprinkle with broken pieces of meringue as you go and fold in until it is all combined. Top with a piece of wax paper to limit exposure to air, cover, and freeze until ready to serve.

# PINK GOOSEBERRY AND HAZELNUT CRUNCH

Pink dessert gooseberries are softer and jammier than their green cousins, and combining them with hazelnuts has the familiarity of old-fashioned British desserts like gooseberry crumble.

*For the hazelnut crunch (makes more than you need)*
150 g/⅔ cup freshly ground lightly toasted hazelnuts
100 g/½ cup all-purpose flour, sifted
100 g/½ cup spelt flour, sifted
90 g/½ cup sugar
40 g/¼ cup light brown muscovado sugar
Pinch of sea salt
125 g/1 stick (½ cup) unsalted butter, cubed

*For the ice cream*
400 g/1 lb pink (sometimes called dessert) gooseberries
110 ml/½ cup whole milk
250 ml/1 cup heavy cream
140 g/¾ cup sugar
2 large egg yolks

1. To make the hazelnut crunch: preheat the oven to 350°F and line a baking sheet with parchment.

(recipe continues)

2. Combine all the dry ingredients in a mixing bowl. Add the cubed butter and rub in lightly with your fingertips until the mixture resembles pebbly sand.

3. Sprinkle the mixture evenly over the lined baking sheet and bake until golden and toasty, 20 to 25 minutes. Check the mixture every 10 minutes and turn it if necessary to make sure it cooks evenly. Remove from the oven and leave to cool in a dry place. Once cold, store in a zip-top plastic bag in the freezer until ready to use.

4. To prepare the ice cream: rinse the gooseberries. Don't bother to trim the tops and tails; they get sieved away later. The best way to cook the gooseberries is very lightly in a microwave; add 2 tablespoons of water, cover the bowl with plastic wrap, and cook for 2 to 3 minutes on high. Otherwise, simmer them gently in a non-reactive pan until they are tender and bursting and look milky and opaque (do not boil). Cool in a sink of ice water. Once cold, cover and chill in the fridge.

5. Heat the milk and cream together, stirring every so often. When the liquid reaches a simmer, whisk the egg yolks and the sugar together in a separate bowl until combined.

6. Pour the hot liquid over the yolks in a thin stream, whisking continuously. Return all the mix to the pan and cook over low heat until it reaches 82°C/180°F. Stir constantly to avoid curdling the eggs and keep a close eye on it so as not to let it boil. As soon as your digital thermometer says 82°C/180°F, place the pan in a sink of ice water to cool. Speed up the cooling process by stirring the mix every so often. Once the custard is at room temperature, transfer it into a clean container, cover with plastic wrap, and chill in the fridge.

7. To make the ice cream: the following day, use a spatula to scrape the chilled gooseberries into the custard, then liquidize the two together with an immersion blender until smooth and very pale pink, 2 to 3 minutes. Use a small ladle to push the gooseberry custard through a fine-mesh sieve or chinois to remove the seeds (discard the seeds).

8. Pour the custard into an ice cream machine and churn according to the machine's instructions until frozen and the texture of whipped cream, 20 to 25 minutes.

9. Quickly transfer the ice cream to a lidded container, sprinkling with 50 g/¼ cup of the frozen hazelnut crunch. Top with a piece of wax paper, cover, and freeze until ready to serve.

# MULBERRY GRANITA

If you ever find yourself in Puglia during summertime, hot-foot it to Super Mago del Gelo: a brilliant gelateria in Polignano al Mare, just south of Bari. My dream ice cream shop, it's fitted in dazzling 1970s Italian style, replete with backlit technicolor landscape photography, pin-up Dolce Vita hotties, pleather banquettes, black marble counter, abundant terrazzo, and last but not least, a beautiful candy-striped Perspex ceiling.

Best of all, its handwritten signs advertise *granita di gelso nero*, or black mulberry granita. This heavenly slush of ruby-colored ice crystals comes smothered with barely sweetened whipped cream. It's the best way to enjoy the wonderful flavor of the mulberry fruit in its purest form.

Mulberries aren't easily available, so make friends with anyone you know who has a tree—or start looking into cheap flights to Bari.

450 g/1 lb mulberries
175 g/¾ cup sugar
500 ml/2 cups water
Zest and juice of 1 lemon

1. Place a large shallow stainless steel baking sheet or dish in the freezer to get very cold.

2. Cook the mulberries ever so lightly, just so that they are piping hot all the way through and juicy and burst. If you have a microwave,

(recipe continues)

just zap them in a bowl for a minute or two. Otherwise, heat them in a non-reactive pan just until the fruit bursts (do not boil). Cool them by placing the pan or bowl in a sink of ice water. Cover and chill in the fridge.

3. Once the berries are cold, blitz them with the sugar, water, and lemon zest until very smooth and the sugar granules have dissolved, 2 to 3 minutes. Use a small ladle to push this mixture through a fine-mesh sieve or chinois to remove the seeds. Add the lemon juice to the mulberry purée and whisk to combine.

4. Pour the liquid into the frozen baking sheet and return it to the freezer, carefully placing it flat on a shelf. Once an hour has passed, check the granita: it should have begun to freeze around the edges. Use a fork to break up any frozen bits and stir them back into the mix.

5. Every 45 minutes, return to stir the granita. Keep agitating it to prevent it from freezing solid. The aim is to achieve large, slushy, frozen crystals.

6. The end result after about 3 hours should be a heap of ruby-red ice crystals. Serve in chilled glasses with softly whipped cream. This can be kept covered in the freezer for up to one week, but you'll need to scrape with a fork before serving to break up any large lumps.

# FAKE MULBERRY

Mulberries reign supreme over all berries—they are one of the greatest-tasting fruits on earth—but they are also difficult to get hold of (literally). Even if you find a tree, too often the fruits have been picked clean by birds or greedy hands—and its Murphy's law that the superior, blackest berries you want are always out of reach. Ripe mulberries are also so fragile they explode with juice before you can tweak them from the branch—leaving you slurping purple streaks from your outstretched arms, but with your hands empty.

A remarkable discovery was when I realized that steeping mulberry leaves in sugar syrup re-creates the distinct earth-and-rain flavor of the berries almost perfectly. Once you mix the flavored syrup with a tart berry (tayberries are perfect because of their less recognizable flavor, but raspberries or blackberries work, too), then, apart from the irreplaceable ruby color, you can be fooled into thinking you've got the real thing. Needless to say, if you can use real mulberries in this recipe then you would be crackers not to.

8 fresh mulberry leaves
190 g/1 cup sugar
240 ml/1 cup water
450 g/1 lb raspberries, blackberries, or tayberries
Juice of 1 lemon

1. To prepare the sorbet: rinse the mulberry leaves (check for silkworms). Stack them on a chopping board and roll them up into a cigar shape, then slice them into ribbons.

2. Heat the sugar and 190 ml/¾ cup of the water together in a pan to make a simple syrup, stirring to dissolve the grains of sugar. As soon as the syrup comes to a boil, add the mulberry leaf ribbons and stir to submerge. Cover the pan tightly with plastic wrap and set in a sink of ice water to infuse for 40 minutes.

3. Strain the syrup, squeezing every drop from the leaves. Discard the leaves, then cover and chill the syrup in the fridge.

4. Lightly cook the berries. If you have a microwave, just zap them in a bowl for a minute or two, until the fruit is very lightly cooked. If not, cook them together in a non-reactive pan just until the berries burst. Cool in a sink of ice water, then chill in the fridge.

5. To make the sorbet: once everything is cold, blitz the berries, syrup, and lemon juice together with a blender until very smooth, 2 to 3 minutes. Pass this purée through a fine-mesh sieve or chinois to remove the seeds. Wash the seeds by rinsing them in the sieve over a bowl with the remaining 50 ml/¼ cup water. Add the pip seed juice to the purée and whisk to combine.

6. Pour the sorbet mix into an ice cream machine and churn according to the machine's instructions until frozen, thick, and creamy-looking, usually 20 to 25 minutes.

7. Scrape the sorbet into a suitable lidded container. Top with a piece of wax paper to limit exposure to air, cover, and freeze until ready to serve.

# YELLOW PEACH AND BASIL

I like sorbet, but unless it's a scorching hot day, I like it best with a scoop of ice cream or a spoonful of whipped cream on the side, not only because the combination of fresh fruit and sweet grassy cream is a winner, but because I live in England where we need the extra calories of cream to keep us warm. Realistically, it's only really hot enough to tolerate ice-cold frozen fruit about three days a year.

This sorbet is destined for one of those days. It's best made with those big, rich peaches with highlighter-yellow flesh—the kind used for tinned peaches (sometimes called Percoche or clingstone).

Oddly, for such a bold-tasting herb as basil, combining it with peach creates such a wonderful synthesis of flavors—you almost don't notice that it's there. Instead, you wonder whether this is the way that ripe peaches are always supposed to taste—like warm skin in the sun, and Italy and summer holidays.

160 g/¾ cup sugar
160 ml/¾ cup water
40 g/2 oz basil leaves
525 g/1½ lb ripe yellow peach (about 3 large peaches)
Zest and juice of 1 lemon, preferably unwaxed

1. To prepare the sorbet: put the sugar and water into a small pan and bring to a gentle simmer to make a simple syrup. The moment it simmers, remove it from the heat and stir in the basil leaves to submerge. Cover the pan tightly with plastic wrap and place it in a sink of ice water, allowing the basil to steep in the cooling syrup.

2. Taste the syrup after 15 minutes; it should taste warmly fragrant with basil. If necessary, steep for a further 5 minutes to boost the flavor before testing again. Do not leave it for more than 30 minutes in total—basil is a "wet" herb, and it will begin to taste weedy if left to stew in the syrup for too long.

3. Strain the syrup into a clean container using a fine-mesh sieve or chinois. Squeeze hard on the basil to extract as much flavor as possible, then discard the basil leaves.

4. Rinse the peaches and slice them roughly into the basil syrup. Add the lemon zest and juice, then cover and chill in the fridge overnight.

5. To make the sorbet: the following day, remove the syrupy peaches from the fridge and liquidize for 2 minutes until very smooth. Pass the mixture through a fine-mesh sieve or chinois, discarding the skin.

6. Pour the bright yellow purée into an ice cream machine and churn according to the machine's instructions until frozen and thick and creamy-looking, usually 20 to 25 minutes.

7. Transfer the sorbet to a suitable lidded container. Top with a piece of wax paper to limit exposure to air, cover, and freeze until ready to serve. Best eaten within 2 weeks.

# MELON AND JASMINE

Italian delis always have a particular warm, dry, baby's-head smell of egg pasta and Parmesan. Mini-markets in the South of France during July and August smell headily of overripe charentais melon. Happily this means that each time I eat pasta and cheese or a slice of ripe charentais melon I get that same blissful feeling of being on holiday.

Using fresh jasmine to flavor this sorbet is totally over the top, but it's a good way to live life to excess. You can pick blossoms from a garden or buy inexpensive flowering plants from many supermarkets—rinse them first, though, in this case—or just use jasmine tea. Serve with Fig Leaf Milk Ice (page 65) or a plain almond ice cream made using the Pistachio ice cream recipe as a base (page 176).

125 g/⅔ cup sugar
125 ml/⅔ cup water
Large handful of jasmine (about 20 g/1 oz blossoms)
or 2 tablespoons loose jasmine tea
½ teaspoon citric acid
1 small ripe melon (charentais or cantaloupe)
Juice of 1½ lemons

(recipe continues)

1. To make the jasmine syrup: bring the sugar and water to a boil in a medium pan, stirring occasionally to make sure the sugar dissolves. Place the pan in a sink full of ice water to cool.

2. Pour the cool syrup into a clean lidded container, then stir in the jasmine blossoms to submerge. Cover the syrup at surface level with a layer of plastic wrap. (This is so that no air can get in—to avoid oxidization of the jasmine.) Place a tight-fitting lid on the container and chill in the fridge for 4 to 5 days.

3. After the elapsed time, strain the syrup through a fine-mesh sieve or chinois, squeezing hard to extract as much flavor as possible from the blossoms. Discard the jasmine and whisk the citric acid into the syrup until dissolved. Keep in the fridge or freeze until needed.

4. To prepare the sorbet: peel the melon, trimming away all the green parts. Don't bother to deseed it. Slice into chunks over a bowl to catch the juice.

5. Add the lemon juice and jasmine syrup to the melon, as well as any of the juice. Liquidize until very smooth, 2 minutes. Use a small ladle to push the purée through a fine-mesh sieve or chinois and discard the seeds.

6. To make the sorbet: pour the melon purée into an ice cream machine and churn according to the machine's instructions until frozen and thick and creamy-looking, usually 20 to 25 minutes.

7. Transfer the sorbet to a suitable lidded container. Top with a piece of wax paper to limit exposure to air, cover, and freeze until ready to serve.

Variation—Replace the jasmine blossoms with a tablespoon of oolong tea leaves and make a cooling Melon and Oolong sorbet. Bring the sugar syrup to a boil and then allow it to cool for a couple of minutes before stirring in the tea leaves. Leave these to steep for 5 minutes then strain the syrup. Cool and chill the oolong syrup and proceed as above.

# BLACKBERRY AND ROSE GERANIUM

Sometimes called "poor man's rose," rose geranium grows pretty happily anywhere there's light. I gave a couple of pinched cuttings to Mr. Piddington, my ice cream shed next-door neighbor. He has the most vigorous front garden in the street thanks to spending the greater part of his weekly state pension on Miracle-Gro.

Within a couple of months the plants were shoulder height and busting through the iron railings. Brushing the leaves with the edge of my jacket as I walk past every day releases fumes of what seems like essence of Turkish delight. Capturing this flavor and combining it with wild blackberries makes a wondrous sorbet—as delicious as (free) frozen fruit and water can get.

I like to freeze the churned sorbet in ice-pop molds, and once they're hard frozen, dip them in thick melted milk chocolate before refreezing.

150 g/¾ cup sugar
200 ml/¾ cup water
6 rose geranium leaves
400 g/1 lb blackberries, wild if possible
Juice of 1 lemon

(recipe continues)

1. To prepare the sorbet: heat the sugar and 150 ml/⅔ cup of the water together in a pan to make a simple syrup, stirring to dissolve the grains of sugar. As soon as the syrup comes to a boil, stir in the rose geranium leaves. Cover tightly with plastic wrap and set in a sink of ice water to infuse for 30 minutes. Once cold, chill in the fridge with the leaves still in the syrup.

2. Lightly cook the blackberries. If using a microwave, place them in a heatproof bowl with a tablespoon of water, cover the bowl with plastic wrap, and cook on high for 2 to 3 minutes. Otherwise, simmer them gently in a non-reactive pan just until they are collapsed and piping hot (do not boil). Cool the bowl in a sink of ice water, then cover and chill in the fridge.

3. To make the sorbet: remove the syrup from the fridge and strain it over the blackberries, squeezing every drop from the geranium leaves. Discard the leaves and add the lemon juice to the fruit.

4. Blitz the blackberries, syrup, and lemon juice together until very smooth, 2 to 3 minutes. Pass this purée through a fine-mesh sieve or chinois to remove the seeds. Wash the seeds by straining the remaining 50 ml/3 tablespoons water over them then add this pip juice to the blackberry purée.

5. Pour the sorbet mix into an ice cream machine and churn according to the machine's instructions until frozen, thick, and creamy-looking, usually 20 to 25 minutes.

6. Scrape the sorbet into a suitable lidded container. Top with a piece of wax paper to limit exposure to air, cover, and freeze until ready to serve.

# APRICOT AND ROSE PETAL

This is a romantic kind of sorbet to make in midsummer, when the apricots (of your dreams) are overripe and the roses are blowsy (or the blouses are rosy). Look for pink-blushed fruits that dent like memory foam when you press them. The more deeply orange the insides the better—they make a wild-colored sorbet.

This recipe calls for rose petals to steep in sugar syrup for a week to capture their delicate fragrance. If you don't have the time, substitute shop-bought rose water or syrup (see page 226), but the scent you get from fresh petals is the best, particularly in combination with apricots—like taking a deep sniff from an armful of flowers.

*For the rose petal syrup* (makes more than you need)
160 g/¾ cup sugar
160 ml/¾ cup water
50 g fresh/2 oz scented rose petals (organic, not sprayed)
¼ teaspoon citric acid

*For the sorbet*
525 g/1 lb 3 oz ripe apricots (about 12 large apricots)
260 ml/1 cup rose petal syrup
Juice of ½ lemon

1. To make the syrup: bring the sugar and water to a simmer in a medium pan, stirring occasionally to make sure the sugar dissolves. Place the pan in a sink of ice water to cool.

2. Pour the cool syrup into a clean lidded container, then stir the rose petals in to submerge. Cover the syrup at surface level with a layer of plastic wrap. Do this so that no air can get in, to avoid oxidization of the rose petals. Place a tightly fitting lid on the container and chill in the fridge for 1 week.

3. After a week, strain the syrup through a fine-mesh sieve or chinois, squeezing hard to extract as much flavor as possible from the petals. Discard the petals and whisk the citric acid into the syrup to dissolve. The syrup can be stored in a clean glass bottle or jar in the fridge for up to a week (or it can be frozen in a suitable container).

4. To prepare the sorbet: slice the apricots in half and remove the pits. Cook the apricots very lightly just until the fruit collapses. If using a microwave, place the fruit in a heatproof bowl with a tablespoon of water. Cover the bowl with plastic wrap and cook on high for 2 to 3 minutes until tender. Otherwise, simmer the apricot halves gently in a non-reactive pan just until they are cooked through and piping hot (do not boil). Cool in a sink of ice water, then cover and chill in the fridge until completely cold, 2 to 3 hours.

5. Carefully measure out 260 ml/1 cup rose petal syrup. Add this to the apricots along with the lemon juice and liquidize them together for 2 minutes, until very smooth. Pass the mixture through a fine-mesh sieve or chinois, discarding the skin.

6. To make the sorbet: pour the apricot purée into an ice cream machine and churn according to the machine's instructions until frozen and thick and creamy-looking, usually 20 to 25 minutes.

7. Transfer the sorbet to a suitable lidded container. Top with a piece of wax paper to limit exposure to air, cover, and freeze until ready to serve. Best eaten within 2 weeks.

Note—Alternatively, make the syrup using 160 g/¾ cup sugar plus 100 ml/½ cup water and 2 tablespoons of rose water.

# PÊCHE DE VIGNE

Elizabeth David wrote once about being served a perfect *Pêche de Vigne* for dessert in a restaurant in Paris in the 1940s—cygnet gray skin concealing sharp raspberry-rose fleshed fruit within. It came presented in its own box: lined with black satin and sitting on a pink velvet cushion. It was the speciality of a town called Montreuil.

From the sixteenth century onward, *pêches sanguines* (blood peaches) were trained to grow in the walled fruit gardens of Montreuil along a maze of sun-trapped bricks. These gardens are peach-less now but still exist—I looked them up!

Here in my flat in Elephant and Castle my heart actually aches for a walled fruit garden. You too may spend an unreasonable amount of time dreaming about moving to Montreuil to open a Pêche de Vigne ice cream kiosk after tasting this ice cream ...

4 or 5 ripe Pêche de Vigne or blood peaches (alternatively use 4 regular peaches and 100 g/4 oz fresh raspberries, about 650 g/1½ lb total weight)
Zest and juice of 1 lemon, preferably unwaxed
1 teaspoon raspberry vinegar (optional)
210 g/1 cup sugar
150 ml/¾ cup whole milk
350 ml/1¼ cups heavy cream
Pinch of sea salt
4 egg yolks

1. To prepare the ice cream: cut an X in the bottom of each peach and then lower them into boiling water for about 20 seconds. Dip the peaches into cold water again to refresh them, and then let them cool. The skins should slip right off (see Note).

2. Halve the peeled peaches, collecting any juice in a bowl underneath. Remove the pit, quarter, and roughly chop the fruit into the bowl. Add the lemon zest and the juice, the raspberry vinegar (if using), and 50 g/¼ cup of the sugar. Stir gently, cover with plastic wrap, and leave to macerate in the fridge.

3. Bring the milk, cream, and salt to a simmer in a non-reactive pan. Stir often, using a whisk or silicone spatula, to prevent it from catching. Once the liquid is hot and steaming, whisk the egg yolks and the rest of the sugar together in a separate bowl until combined.

4. Pour the hot liquid over the yolks in a thin stream, whisking continuously. Return all the mix to the pan and cook over low heat until it reaches 82°C/180°F. Stir constantly to avoid curdling the eggs and keep a close eye on it so as not to let it boil. As soon as your digital thermometer says 82°C/180°F, place the pan in a sink of ice water to cool. Speed up the cooling process by stirring the mix every so often. Once the custard is at room temperature, transfer it into a clean container, cover with plastic wrap, and chill.

5. To make the ice cream: the following day, use a spatula to scrape the chilled peaches into the custard, then liquidize until as smooth as possible. Using a small ladle, push the peach custard through a fine-mesh sieve or chinois into a clean container.

6. Pour the custard into an ice cream machine and churn according to the machine's instructions until frozen and the texture of whipped cream, usually 20 to 25 minutes.

7. Transfer the ice cream to a suitable lidded container. Top with a piece of wax paper to limit exposure to air, cover, and freeze until ready to serve.

Note—Pêche de Vigne is an old-fashioned variety of peach. It has thick, fuzzy skin that has been bred out of more modern cultivars. You need to remove this, otherwise it will spoil the finished texture of the ice cream.

You can replace the Pêche de Vigne with Nectarine de Vigne for an equally delicious ice cream: simply rinse, slice, and macerate—no need to peel.

## Fig Leaves

Figs—at least ones grown in this country—usually need the protection of a walled garden and a good couple of weeks' consistent warmth to get their juices going and to give the fruit a chance of ripening properly. Fig leaves have a gorgeous smell, though, whatever the weather, and can be used to impart flavor in lots of ways in the kitchen. If you keep your eyes peeled, you'll see the trees growing in all sorts of places.

I was once told that fig trees flourish near water sources within Victorian towns, and have noticed this to be true as I often see them growing near canals and small streams in places like London and Cambridge. The reason for this is supposed to be that the seeds of dried figs (having been eaten and then...um...passed) make their way through old sewage systems then out to the countryside until they find a likely-looking place to germinate.

Cycling through St. James's Park on a sunny afternoon, by the lake that leads up to Buckingham Palace, I was stopped in my tracks quite literally by the warm smell of figs. Towering over the pelicans, and figgier than a £60 candle, grew a... majestic tree. Could it be the consequence of a fantastic box of Turkish figs enjoyed by Queen Victoria many Christmases ago? I picked a modest few of its lovely leaves to make my first fig leaf ice cream, and have been doing so ever since. Now's the time to admit this—forgive me, Your Majesty.

# FIG LEAF AND RASPBERRY

Raspberries provide the acidity and brightness necessary to complement fig leaves' soft, dusky flavor. Try serving this alongside Pigeon Fig and Pineau des Charentes (page 66) or Green Walnut ice cream (page 144).

2 fresh fig leaves
190 g/1 cup sugar
240 ml/1 cup water
450 g/1 lb raspberries
Juice of 1 lemon

1. To prepare the sorbet: rinse the fig leaves and cut out the core stem. Stack the leaves, roll them up, and cut them into wide ribbons.

2. Heat the sugar and 190 ml/¾ cup of the water together in a pan to make a simple syrup, stirring to dissolve the sugar. As soon as the syrup comes to a boil, add the sliced fig leaves. Cover tightly with plastic wrap and set in a sink of ice water to infuse for 40 minutes.

3. Strain the syrup, squeezing every drop from the leaves. Discard the leaves and add the syrup and raspberries to a bowl. Either microwave the mix for a minute or two or cook together in a non-reactive pan just until the raspberries burst. Cool in a sink of ice water.

4. Liquidize the raspberries and lemon juice until very smooth. Pass this purée through a fine-mesh sieve or chinois to remove the seeds. Rinse the seeds with the remaining 50 ml/¼ cup water, add this pip juice to the purée, and whisk to combine. Cover and refrigerate.

5. To make the sorbet: remove the purée from the fridge and whisk well to combine, in case it has separated slightly. Pour the sorbet mix into an ice cream machine and churn according to the machine's instructions until frozen, 20 to 25 minutes.

6. Scrape the sorbet into a suitable lidded container. Top with a piece of wax paper, cover, and freeze until ready to serve.

# Green Walnuts

One stormy spring day in Lambeth, I discovered a big old walnut tree growing behind the council garage where I park my ice cream van. Typically, I smelled the tree first with my constantly alert, food-seeking hooter, before looking up and noticing it. A few of its unripe nuts had been blown onto the concrete forecourt and after being reversed over and crushed a few times by my Piaggio Ape, had scented the air with a deliciously spicy zephyr. Before you could say Squirrel Nutkins, I persuaded my long-suffering husband to scuttle up the tree and pick a carrier bagful to take back to the ice cream shed.

# Nocino Liqueur

In Italy, tender green (or unripe) walnuts are traditionally harvested in midsummer to make dark, espresso-colored nocino and have to be picked before the shell has had time to form. If you want to be really precise about it, they ought to be plucked from the tree by barefoot maidens on the eve of the feast of St. John the Baptist (June 24). The walnut has always maintained an aura of legend in Italy, linked to the presence of witches and spells, and happily the alchemy would seem to be transmitted into this bewitching elixir.

To make your own nocino, fill a clean 2-liter bottling jar (or two 1-liter jars) with a liter of cheap vodka, 500 g/2 cups sugar, 10 cloves, 2 cinnamon sticks, ½ teaspoon black peppercorns, ½ vanilla pod, and strips of zest from one unwaxed lemon. Stir together until the sugar dissolves, then add 30 quartered green walnuts (wear gloves when slicing them—the juice will stain your hands nicotine brown!). Shake the jar gently to expel any air bubbles, then seal it, write the date on the tape, and stick it on the side.

Leave the jar(s) in a sunny, bright spot in your kitchen and turn every few days to expose the walnuts to the light. Continue to do this for 6 weeks. After 6 weeks, strain the walnuts and spices from the liquid, and pass the liquid through coffee filters or a jelly bag into clean bottles. Once your nocino has been bottled, store it out of sight somewhere dark—it musn't be drunk until November 3 at the earliest, and gets darker and more delicious the longer you leave it.

Sip it as a curative *digestivo* after heavy winter dinners, pour it over vanilla ice cream as you would with *affogato*, or, best of all, use it to make ice cream.

Fig Leaf and Raspberry (page 141) / Green Walnut (page 144) / Pigeon Fig and Pineau des Charentes (page 66)

# GREEN WALNUT

This is one of my very favorite ice creams. The flavors echo maple, butterscotch, and espresso but are resolutely unique. It would be the one to serve at a banquet (if you ever had a banquet)—a perfect accompaniment to Fig Leaf and Raspberry sorbet (page 141) and Pigeon Fig and Pineau des Charentes ice cream (page 66).

300 ml/1¼ cups whole milk
300 ml/1¼ cups heavy cream
6 egg yolks
90 g/½ cup sugar
4 candied green walnuts, drained and chopped
(about half a 450 g/1 lb jar)
3 tablespoons nocino liqueur

1. To prepare the ice cream: heat the milk and heavy cream in a non-reactive pan. Stir often, using a whisk or silicone spatula, to prevent it catching. When the liquid is steaming hot, whisk the egg yolks and sugar together in a separate bowl until combined.

2. Pour the hot milk and cream over the yolks in a thin stream, whisking continuously. Return all the mix to the pan and cook over low heat until it reaches 82°C/180°F, stirring all the time to avoid curdling the eggs and keeping a close eye on it so as not to let it boil. As soon as your digital thermometer says 82°C/180°F, remove the pan from the heat, add the chopped green walnuts or raw walnuts (see

Note), and blend these into the custard with an immersion blender, then place the pan in a sink of ice water to cool. Stir the custard every so often to help it cool more quickly. Once the custard is at room temperature, stir in the nocino liqueur. Scrape the mixture into a clean container, cover with plastic wrap, and chill in the fridge overnight.

3. To make the ice cream: the following day, use an immersion blender or food processor to blitz the custard again at high speed until very smooth and emulsified, 2 minutes.

4. Pour the custard into an ice cream machine and churn according to the machine's instructions until frozen and the texture of whipped cream, usually 20 to 25 minutes.

5. Scrape the ice cream into a suitable lidded container. Top with a piece of wax paper to limit exposure to air, cover, and freeze until ready to serve.

Note—Look out for jars of fudge-like preserved walnuts (they look like big black olives) in Turkish, Greek, and Middle Eastern shops, where they are known as *ceviz tatlısı* or *glyko karydaki* and are tradition-ally eaten for dessert with *kaymak*—water buffalo clotted cream. Alternatively, you could substitute the candied walnuts for 30 g/1 oz raw shelled walnuts and add an extra 2 tablespoons of nocino liqueur. Nocino or *vin de noix* can be found online.

AGRICOOP
PACHINESE

# WILD FIG AND WATERMELON

I had almost given up on the notion of a watermelon sorbet—why overcomplicate the beauty of an icy slice of ripe watermelon? Then one Indian summer day I found myself with some figs to use up. I couldn't bear to waste them—they were lovely squashed ones I'd picked on holiday in Sardinia but there weren't enough to make fig ice cream or sorbet. I struck upon the idea of using them with watermelon—also plentiful at that time of year.

The figs give body and sap to the watery pink watermelon juice, dulling its color a deep blue-red. It's a wonderfully refreshing but easy-to-scoop sorbet. If you can't pick wild figs I won't hold it against you—just use the ripest, blackest ones you can find.

225 g/½ lb ripe black or Turkish figs (about 6)
700 g/1½ lb watermelon flesh (red part only)
110 g/½ cup sugar
Juice of 1 lemon

1. To prepare the sorbet: rinse the figs then slice in half and place them in a bowl, sprinkled with a tablespoon of water. Cover the bowl with plastic wrap, and cook in a microwave on high for 3 to 4 minutes. Otherwise, simmer them gently in a non-reactive pan just until they're tender, juicy, and piping hot (do not boil). Set aside to cool; once cold, cover and chill in the fridge along with the cubed watermelon flesh (in a separate container) until completely cold, 2 to 3 hours.

(recipe continues)

2. Once the figs are thoroughly chilled, liquidize them with the watermelon, sugar, and lemon juice long enough for the sugar granules to dissolve, 2 to 3 minutes. Use a small ladle to push the purée through a fine-mesh sieve or chinois. Save a couple of teaspoons of the seeds if you like and add these back to the purée for texture.

3. To make the sorbet: pour the dark red purée into an ice cream machine and churn according to the machine's instructions until frozen and thick and creamy-looking, usually 20 to 25 minutes.

4. Transfer the sorbet to a suitable lidded container. Top with a piece of wax paper to limit exposure to air, cover, and freeze until ready to serve. Best eaten within 2 weeks.

# VANILLA PLUM

Plums have a dependable quality I like. Even unripe, unexciting ones—
in fact, even those rock-hard purple tennis balls you get year-round at
the supermarket. They undergo a kind of alchemy once they're cooked
and the tannic depths of flavor are drawn from their skins, becoming
lusty and slurp-able. This makes them a very good choice for ice cream.

Next time you get a glut of wasp-eaten windfalls—or a netted plastic
tub of plums from the supermarket—try making this inexpensive,
sweet, and lovely ice cream. I like it best as part of a triple scoop with
Pêche de Vigne ice cream (page 138) and Pear, Myrtle, and Ginger
sorbet (page 157).

450 g/1 lb plums (varieties like Victoria, Jubilee, Marjorie's Seedling,
and Quetsche d'Alsace are all good)
140 ml/½ cup whole milk
200 ml/1 cup heavy cream
½ vanilla pod, split lengthwise
3 egg yolks
160 g/¾ cup+ 1 tablespoon sugar

1. To prepare the ice cream: cook the plums lightly. If using a microwave,
halve and pit the plums and place them in a heatproof bowl. Cover
the bowl with plastic wrap and cook for 3 to 4 minutes on high. Otherwise simmer them gently in a non-reactive pan just until they
are tender, pulpy, and piping hot (do not boil). Set aside to cool; once
cold, cover and chill in the fridge.

(recipe continues)

2. Heat the milk, cream, and split vanilla pod gently, stirring every so often with a whisk or silicone spatula. When the liquid reaches a simmer, whisk the egg yolks and the sugar together in a separate bowl for a few seconds to combine.

3. Pour the hot liquid over the yolks in a thin stream, whisking continuously. Return all the mix to the pan and cook over low heat until it reaches 82°C/180°F. Stir constantly to avoid curdling the eggs and keep a close eye on it so as not to let it boil. As soon as your digital thermometer says 82°C/180°F, place the pan in a sink of ice water to cool. Speed up the cooling process by stirring the mix every so often. Once the custard is at room temperature, transfer it into a clean container, cover with plastic wrap, and chill in the fridge.

4. To make the ice cream: the following day, pick out the vanilla pod and squeeze out all the little black seeds, adding them back to the custard. Use a spatula to scrape the chilled plums into the custard, making sure there are no bits of pit still attached. Liquidize for 2 to 3 minutes, or until very smooth. Use a small ladle to push the pink custard through a fine-mesh sieve or chinois into a clean container. Discard any remaining seeds and fruit skin.

5. Pour the plum custard into an ice cream machine and churn according to the machine's instructions until frozen and the texture of whipped cream, 20 to 25 minutes.

6. Transfer the ice cream to a suitable lidded container. Top with a piece of wax paper to limit exposure to air, cover, and freeze until ready to serve. Best eaten within a couple of weeks.

Note—If you get a big haul of plums it's worth remembering that they freeze beautifully when halved, pitted, and bagged up in zip-top bags. They can be cooked like this frozen, and will see you through winter with delicious fruity ice cream.

# DAMSON AND GRAPPA

I have adored grappa ever since I was a sad 16-year-old foreign exchange student on a trip to Italy and took to ordering *caffè coretto con grappa* (espresso with grappa) because I thought it was cool and because I discovered it was cheaper to order standing at the bar. (Ah—I miss my teenaged self now.)

Grappa is a grape-based brandy with a high alcohol content. Its flavor catches you at the back of your throat, making you feel breathless and reducing your voice to a husky rasp. It is a natural partner for the deeply dusky damson plum, lightly correcting the fruit's natural dryness.

This is one of the best recipes in the book—it is thick, satiny, and splendid, and has a papal purple color fit for a pair of pope's socks.

300 g/½ lb damson plums
160 ml/⅔ cup whole milk
240 ml/1 cup heavy cream
3 large egg yolks
130 g/⅔ cup sugar
1 tablespoon grappa

Following pages: Choco Ice (page 230) using Damson and Grappa with Almond Nougat (page 224)

1. To prepare the ice cream: rinse the damsons, then slice them in half and pit them. Put them in a bowl and sprinkle a couple of tablespoons of water over the top. Cover the bowl with plastic wrap and cook in a microwave on high for 3 to 4 minutes. Otherwise, simmer them gently in a non-reactive pan just until they're tender, pulpy, and piping hot (do not boil). Set aside to cool; once cold, cover and chill in the fridge.

2. Gently heat the milk and cream, stirring every so often with a whisk or silicone spatula to prevent it from catching. When the liquid reaches a simmer, whisk the egg yolks and the sugar together in a separate bowl for a few seconds to combine.

3. Pour the hot liquid over the yolks in a thin stream, whisking continuously. Return all the mix to the pan and cook over low heat until it reaches 82°C/180°F. Stir constantly to avoid curdling the eggs and keep a close eye on it so as not to let it boil. As soon as your digital thermometer says 82°C/180°F, place the pan in a sink of ice water to cool. Speed up the cooling process by stirring the mix every so often. Once the custard is at room temperature, transfer it to a clean container, cover with plastic wrap, and chill in the fridge.

4. To make the ice cream: the following day, use a spatula to scrape the chilled damsons and any juice into the custard—check that there are no bits of pit still attached. Add the grappa and liquidize for 2 to 3 minutes, or until very smooth. Use a small ladle to push the plum-colored custard through a fine-mesh sieve or chinois into a clean container. Discard any remaining pits and fruit skin.

5. Pour the custard into an ice cream machine and churn according to the machine's instructions until frozen and the texture of whipped cream, about 20 to 25 minutes.

6. Transfer the ice cream to a suitable lidded container. Top with a piece of wax paper to limit exposure to air, cover, and freeze until ready to serve.

Note—If you have a Mouli rotational grater and the damson plums prove too hard to pit, it can be easier to cook the fruit whole, and then pass them through the Mouli when they are done to remove the pits.

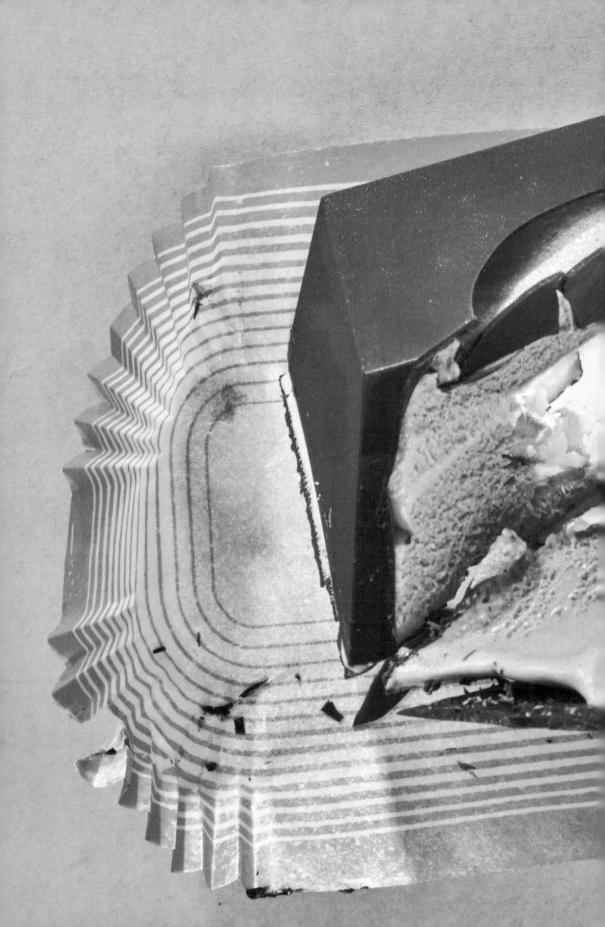

# Prickly Pear

I first saw prickly pears growing in Sardinia; it was late September and the Mediterranean island was a dusty rock by the time we visited. This comical-looking cactus plant, pinned with dabs of sunset fruits and flowers, lined every roadside along with monstrous overgrown fennel, myrtle, figs, olives, and grapes. The vigor of all this wild food growing in the rubble was dazzling and made me feel depressed about my window box.

On the last day of the trip, with the car packed to head back to the airport (I'd filled my luggage with squished figs, newspaper wraps of fennel pollen, and tins of tomatoes), I remembered the prickly pears. The thought of going home without having tried a purple-fleshed *fico d'India* was unthinkable, but—too lazy to do it myself—I persuaded my husband to hop out of the car and pick a couple for me.

"Really?" asked John in a slightly tiresome, anxious way.

"Yes—it's fine! Just twist them off the branch!"

I sat in the car, passenger windows wide open to the late afternoon sun, and watched as Johnny, silhouetted in front of me, plucked a couple of fruits from a high paddle-shaped palm. As the plant pinged back, it released an infinitesimal cloud of needle-like microscopic hairs. They drifted across the sky, settling over a scream-ing John and then on through the car window where I was sat in my shorts—before hooking in to me, too. The shards embedded themselves like fiberglass in very difficult places for several long days before disintegrating. They left me not only with a big grudge against prickly pears, but more than that, with a question: who can be bothered with them and what is the point?

I've tried prickly pear sorbet occasionally since then, tempted back by its extra-ordinary magenta color and wondering if I've missed a trick. The flavor always leaves me nonplussed. It's not that the fruit itself is tasteless—they can be pleasant and somewhat floral, a little like watermelon. But once you add sugar or milk, the delicate flavor is lost. My conclusion is that the best way to eat them is like they do in Mexico; stuck on a stick by someone wearing gloves, frozen, and then delicately peeled to reveal the sweet, refreshing flesh—a kind of whole fruit ice pop.

# PEAR, MYRTLE, AND GINGER

*Pears are gorgeous little beasts, but they're ripe for half an hour, and you're never there...*

This quote from Eddie Izzard pretty much sums up how I feel about pears. My best advice is to buy a couple of the ripest ones you can find, then leave them in a brown paper bag on a high shelf where they can lie untouched and in the dark for three or four days.

Follow your nose here: rather than squeezing and bruising the pears, go for the absolute strongest white-pear-drop smelling ones. Although this is still not a guaranteed tip, as there is always the possibility that you will forget about them and they will implode, the core turning to brown mush while your back is turned. But it is my only one!

With some luck your efforts will be successful and you will be rewarded with this soft, fiery sorbet that hums with pear flavor and has a luxuriant, snowy texture like the center of a fondant crème.

Myrtle is probably easier to find than you think—it's a brushy shrub with small evergreen leaves and starry white flowers. Often planted in hedges and gardens, it has a fragrance a bit like bay, only sweeter and spicier. If you can't find it, it can be left out or replaced with a couple of bay leaves.

Serve with Ricotta and Canditi ice cream (page 213) or make a Pear Colonel—a scoop of sorbet with a shot of frozen Poire Williams (pear brandy) poured over the top.

125 g/⅔ cup sugar
275 ml/1 cup water
3 ripe pears (about 540 g/1¼ lb total weight)
25 g/1 oz freshly picked myrtle leaves
Juice of 1 lemon
8 cm/3-inch piece of fresh ginger

(recipe continues)

1. Put the sugar and the water into a non-reactive pan. Heat gently until the sugar dissolves.

2. Wash the pears and peel them so their peelings and any juice drop directly into the warm syrup. Quarter the pears, cut the cores away from the flesh, and slip the quarters into the syrup along with the myrtle leaves. The pears brown quickly after being exposed to the air, but if they are immersed in the syrup you won't need to hold them in acidulated water beforehand (which can make them soggy).

3. Increase the heat and cover the pears and myrtle with a circle of baking paper (a cloche). Simmer the fruit very gently for a couple of minutes, until the pears are opaque and piping hot all the way through. (Lightly cooking the pears kills the enzyme that makes them go brown.) Cooking them too much will spoil the fresh flavor, so this is to be done with care.

4. Scoop the pear quarters out of the pan and into a clean bowl. Add the lemon juice and then strain the syrup over them, squeezing hard to extract as much flavor as possible. Throw away the peelings and myrtle leaves. Leave to cool then cover and chill in the fridge.

5. To make the sorbet: grate the ginger (I love my microplane) into a small bowl or dish. With clean hands, squeeze the juice out of the grated ginger and add it to the pears (throw away the tough fibers).

6. Blitz the pears, syrup, ginger, and lemon juice with an immersion blender until very smooth. Push the resulting purée through a fine-mesh sieve or chinois.

7. Pour the mix into an ice cream machine and churn according to the machine's instructions or until frozen and thick and snowy, usually 20 to 25 minutes.

8. Scrape the sorbet into a suitable lidded container. Top with a piece of wax paper to limit exposure to air, cover, and freeze until ready to serve.

<hr />

Note—Much of the aroma of apples and pears is contained in their skins. Steeping the pear peelings with the sugar syrup releases some of this essence and improves the flavor of the finished sorbet.

# BRAMLEY APPLE AND BAY LEAF

A gently aromatic ice cream with spice from fresh glossy bay leaves, a little acidity from the apple, and a bite of dark crispness from the buttery rye bread crumbs at the end.

It's slightly discouraging that customers almost always mishear this flavor for one containing Baileys (as in the Irish cream liqueur) rather than bay leaves. I've gotten used to their disappointed reactions. But what can you do? You can't always go with the money.

*For the rye crumbs*
2 slices of 100% rye sourdough bread (preferably a few days old)
1 tablespoon unsalted butter
1 tablespoon soft brown muscovado sugar

*For the ice cream*
1 extra-large Bramley apple (about 400 g/12 oz total weight)
150 ml/½ cup whole milk
200 ml/1 cup heavy cream
3 egg yolks
150 g/¾ cup sugar
6 fresh bay leaves roughly chopped

1. To make the rye crumbs: trim the crusts from the rye bread, tear the slices into pieces, and put these into a food processor and grind them into coarse bread crumbs. Tip into a heavy-based pan and gently toast the crumbs over medium-low heat for 5 to 6 minutes, or until they have dried out somewhat.

2. Add the butter and sugar to the pan. Once it melts, stir it into the bread crumbs so they start to fry and caramelize at the same time. Fry them for another 5 minutes, or until they are crisp. Remove them from the heat and pour onto a piece of parchment to cool in an even layer. Once cold, store them in a zip-top bag in the freezer.

3. To prepare the ice cream: I like cooking Bramleys in a microwave: score a circular line around the stem end and the flower end (see page 18) with a sharp knife, then place the apple in a Pyrex bowl or jug with a tablespoon of water, cover with plastic wrap, and cook for 4 to 5 minutes on medium-high. The apple, if ripe, should explode into fluffy purée. Once it has cooled down you will find it's easy to scrape the cooked apple from the skin and core with a spoon. Otherwise peel, core, and slice the apple and simmer gently in a non-reactive pan with a tablespoon of water, just until it's soft and tender. Leave to cool, then measure out 300 g/12 oz cooked apple into a clean container, cover, and chill in the fridge.

4. Heat the milk and cream together in a pan, stirring every so often with a whisk or silicone spatula to prevent it from catching. When the liquid reaches a simmer, whisk the egg yolks and the sugar together in a separate bowl until combined.

5. Pour the hot liquid over the yolks in a thin stream, whisking continuously. Return all the mix to the pan and cook over low heat until it reaches 82°C/180°F. Stir constantly to avoid curdling the eggs and keep a close eye on it so as not to let it boil. As soon as your digital thermometer says 82°C/180°F, remove from the heat and stir in the fresh bay leaves. Cover the pan with plastic wrap and place the pan in a sink of ice water to cool. Once the custard is at room temperature, scrape it (along with the bay leaves) into a clean container, cover with plastic wrap, and chill in the fridge.

6. To make the ice cream: the following day, strain the custard over the apple purée, discard the bay leaves, and liquidize the custard and apple with an immersion blender until very smooth, 2 minutes. Use a small ladle to push the custard through a fine-mesh sieve or chinois into a clean container.

7. Pour the apple custard into an ice cream machine and churn according to the machine's instructions until frozen and the texture of whipped cream, 20 to 25 minutes.

8. Working quickly, scrape the ice cream into a suitable lidded container, sprinkling with spoonfuls of frozen buttery rye crumbs as you go until you think you've used enough. Top with a piece of wax paper to limit exposure to air, cover, and freeze until ready to serve. Best eaten within about 10 days, while the crumbs are still crisp.

# UVA FRAGOLA

This electric mauve "grape color" sorbet bursts with crazy bubblegum-flavored fruit. *Uva fragola* are a seasonal Italian grape variety similar to Concord grapes, with an intoxicating smell and flavor.

I love this flavor blended with ice and prosecco. Otherwise, it is best served with a creamy scoop of peanut ice cream made like pistachio ice cream, but with toasted peanuts substituted for pistachio nuts (page 177), PB&J style.

550 g/1¼ lb uva fragola or Concord grapes, washed
½ small green or unripe lemon, finely diced
1 teaspoon vitamin C powder
150 g/¾ cup sugar
200 ml/¾ cup water

1. To prepare the sorbet: rinse the grapes and pick from the stem. Put the grapes, diced whole lemon, vitamin C powder, sugar, and water in a bowl and blitz together roughly with an immersion blender. Cover the bowl and chill in the fridge overnight.

2. To make the sorbet: the following day, thoroughly liquidize the grapes (around 3 minutes), making sure any sugar granules have been dissolved and the mixture looks smooth.

3. Pass this mix through a fine-mesh sieve or chinois. Use the back of a ladle to squeeze as much flavor as possible from the skins. When the skins look dry you are done and they can be discarded.

4. Pour the grape purée into an ice cream machine and churn according to the machine's instructions, 20 to 25 minutes.

5. Scrape the sorbet into a suitable lidded container. Top with a piece of wax paper to limit exposure to air, cover, and freeze until ready to serve. Eat within about 2 weeks.

Note—The use of vitamin C powder (you can find it at the pharmacy) draws the strong flavor out of the thick grape skins and prevents the blended fruit from oxidizing and turning brown.

# CRÈME CARAMEL

This recipe is adapted from a creation by the French pastry chef Pierre Hermé, who was a good friend of Lionel Poilâne. I bought Pierre Hermé a box of Poilâne apple tarts one day and in return he gave me a copy of his book *Desserts*, which is where I first read about this rather unusual method of cooking an ice cream base. The base is gently oven-baked to a set custard, then cooled and blended to re-liquefy. It's not an exaggeration to say it transforms it into the richest, silkiest ice cream base ever—the staff at St. John Bread & Wine would mass around like a swarm of bees when it came to scooping the churned stuff out of the machine—I never saw it cleaned so fast.

If you can leave the ice cream a week or so in the freezer it becomes even more irresistible—the shards of crunchy burned sugar melting and pooling into rivulets of liquid caramel.

*For the caramel* (makes more than you need, but it keeps!)
200 g/1 cup superfine sugar

*For the ice cream*
1 vanilla pod
200 ml/¾ cup whole milk
300 ml/1¼ cups heavy cream
55 g/⅓ cup sugar
Pinch of sea salt
5 egg yolks
55 g/¼ cup soft brown unrefined sugar

1. To make the caramel: sprinkle the bottom of a heavy-based pan with an even layer of the superfine sugar. Place it over medium-high heat and cook slowly and without stirring until it begins to melt and caramelize. Swirl the pan to achieve even caramelization. If the caramel starts crystallizing, turn the heat to the lowest setting. The sugar will all eventually melt, and get darker and darker in color.

2. Cook the caramel to a dark copper color—it needs to be cooked long enough for the sugar's sweetness to be replaced with dark caramel flavor, usually a second or two after it begins to smoke.

3. As soon as you reach this stage, carefully pour out the caramel onto a large heatproof silicone mat or onto buttered waxed paper and leave to cool until hardened. Once cold, place the caramel in a sealable airtight bag.

4. To prepare the ice cream: preheat the oven to 275°F.

5. Split the vanilla pod using the tip of a sharp knife, scrape out the seeds, then add both seeds and pod to a pan along with the milk, cream, sugar, and salt. Bring to a simmer over medium heat, whisking often to prevent it from catching. Once the liquid is hot and steaming, whisk the egg yolks and brown sugar together in a separate bowl until combined.

6. Pour the hot milk mix over the yolks in a thin stream, whisking continuously. Pour this mix into a shallow baking sheet, ideally about 24 × 30 cm/9 x 12 inches. Transfer the tray to the oven and bake very gently until just set in the middle but still wobbly (don't worry if the edges are a little more cooked), 20 to 25 minutes, depending on the depth of your pan.

7. Remove the custard from the oven, pick out the vanilla pod, scrape the mixture into a blender, and whizz until smooth and liquid again. Strain the mix through a fine-mesh sieve or chinois, then chill in the fridge.

8. To make the ice cream: the following day, remove the custard from the fridge and blend with an immersion blender for a minute to re-liquefy. Pour the custard into an ice cream machine and churn according to the machine's instructions until frozen and the texture of whipped cream, 20 to 25 minutes.

9. While the ice cream is churning, lightly smash the bag of caramel into smithereens with a rolling pin.

10. Scrape the ice cream into a suitable lidded container, sprinkling with spoonfuls of the smashed caramel as you go. Top with a piece of wax paper to limit exposure to air, cover, and freeze until ready to serve. Best kept a few days in the freezer before eating.

# POMEGRANATE AND BITTER ORANGE GRANITA

In Turkey and the Middle East in the autumn and through winter, it's normal to find street vendors selling fresh, foaming pomegranate juice by the glass (or plastic bagful). You will usually be given the luxury of choosing between two types: sweet and sour. The pressed juice isn't clear and berry red like the expensive stuff you buy in the supermarket; until it settles it has the cloudiness of an unpolished garnet. The flavor cannot be duplicated: it's the most deep, dry, grown-up juice.

Combined with Seville orange juice it makes an invigorating granita that tastes like something from the underworld, and can be tempered just slightly by smothering in zest-spiked, sweetened whipped cream.

65 g/⅓ plus 2 tablespoons sugar (or up to 30% more if using sour pomegranate)

65 ml/¼ cup water

1 Seville orange, leafy orange, or *chinotto* (or use 1 large normal orange)

2 large pomegranates

1. Place a large, shallow stainless steel baking sheet or dish into the freezer to get very cold.

2. Heat the sugar and water together, stir to dissolve the sugar granules, and bring the syrup to a simmer.

3. Rinse the orange, then zest it directly into the hot syrup. Set aside to cool.

4. Cut the pomegranates in half horizontally, then hold each half cut-side down over a large bowl. Bash the curved side of the fruit with a rolling pin until the seeds tumble out between your fingers and into the bowl. Pick out and discard any pieces of pith.

5. Once the syrup is cold, pour it over the seeds with the juice of the orange and liquidize everything together until as smooth as possible, 2 to 3 minutes. Use a small ladle to push this mixture through a fine-mesh sieve or chinois to remove the pomegranate seeds.

6. Pour this mix into the cold baking sheet, and place it flat on a freezer shelf. Stir with a fork after the first hour, then again every subsequent 45 minutes, paying particular attention to the outer edges to prevent hard lumps from forming.

7. The end result after about 3 hours should be a heap of garnet-colored ice crystals. Serve in chilled glasses with softly whipped cream. Can be kept covered in the freezer for up to a week.

Note—When shopping for pomegranates it's not easy to tell which are sweet or sour just from looking, so taste the seeds when you get home and adjust the recipe according to what you've bought. In any case, look for fruits with round, shiny skin as tight as a drum, as though chilblained. Fresh ones should crack open with the pressure of a knife the same way ripe watermelons do.

# SHEEP'S MILK YOGURT AND WILDFLOWER HONEY

This recipe isn't a low-fat alternative to ice cream; it is delicious in its own right, tasting clearly of tangy sheep's milk yogurt and rich, floral wildflower honey.

Yogurt has a much lower fat content than cream, which can make frozen yogurts thin and gritty. But sheep's milk is higher in protein and fat than cow's—when it's the thick, strained kind, more so. Protein adds body to the ice cream, improving the texture and adding structure without the need for fillers like dry milk powder (a staple of most commercial frozen yogurts).

Raw honey is added for flavor and scoop-ability. Serve with Pomegranate and Bitter Orange Granita (page 166) and Quince Custard ice cream (page 173).

550 g/2½ cups strained, full-fat sheep's milk yogurt
30 g/2 tablespoons raw wildflower honey
70 g/⅓ cup sugar
¼ teaspoon iota carrageenan (optional; see Note)
100 ml/½ cup whole milk or sheep's milk, chilled

1. To prepare the frozen yogurt: blend the yogurt and honey together using a food processor or an immersion blender until fully combined; chill in the fridge.

2. Whisk the sugar and carrageenan (if using) together in a bowl, then whisk in the cold milk until fully combined and lump-free.

3. Heat the milk mix to the simmering point, whisking frequently to prevent lumps of carrageenan forming—a microwave does this best, as the amounts are so small. Otherwise, use the smallest pan possible and a mini whisk. Leave the mix to cool in a sink or bowl full of ice water. Once the milk gel is cold, scrape it into the yogurt mix and liquidize for a couple of minutes until fully combined. Pass the mix through a sieve to make sure it's lump-free.

4. To make the frozen yogurt: pour the yogurt into an ice cream machine and churn according to the machine's instructions until frozen and creamy-looking, 20 to 25 minutes.

5. Transfer the frozen yogurt to a suitable lidded container. Top with a piece of wax paper to limit exposure to air, cover, and freeze until ready to serve. Eat within a week.

Note—If you're a sucker for the super-smooth texture of soft-serve frozen yogurt (and I can't deny I love it, too) then carrageenan (a gel derived from natural seaweed) can be added to the mix. It makes up somewhat for this ice missing the emulsifying quality of egg yolk, helping to bind the fat and water molecules together to make the ice extra smooth and silky. If you aren't using carrageenan you can replace the milk with cream or half-and-half.

# Quince

A working day on the pig farm in Urbino started at 6 a.m., when I would catch a ride on the blue tractor down the hill to feed the pigs, cows, rabbits, and chickens. Afterward we would sit and have breakfast in the front yard to catch the easterly sun. Coral-colored quince stewed in a pool of juice, served with thick yogurt, followed by bread and butter and honey and several pots of coffee.

The bread was homemade every few days from a starter, or *madre*, kept in a floury wooden dresser. Butter first had to be wiped clean from where the cat had been licking it in the night and then it could be mashed onto the bread with honey. We swapped our homemade *strutto* (lard) for sheep's yogurt with the German couple down the road who had moved to Italy in the 1980s to start making cheese. The quinces were stolen from the neighboring agriturismo—who to Gigia's disgust served Mulino Bianco biscuits for breakfast despite having planted bewitching ornamental trees around the swimming pool, which were heavy with the Naples-gold fruit in October.

Choose quinces whose waxy yellow skin smells intensely of pineapple cubes. Look out for them in the autumn, often sold alongside fresh chestnuts, pomegranates, and unbrined olives.

Quinces are hard work—prepping them requires an effort comparable to chopping wood, but long, slow cooking transforms their oddly spongy flesh into glowing wonder food with the rich fragrance of citrus and apples and pears.

# QUINCE CUSTARD

I like adding chunks of frozen apple pie to this custard base. Serve alongside Sheep's Milk Yogurt and Wildflower Honey ice cream (page 170) or Pomegranate and Bitter Orange Granita (page 166).

Juice of 1 lemon
200 ml/¾ cup water
650 g/1½ lb whole quinces
Zest and juice of 2 clementines
200 ml/¾ cup whole milk
200 ml/1 cup heavy cream
3 large egg yolks
1 tablespoon honey
180 g/1 cup sugar
1 slice of Bramley apple pie, frozen and chopped (optional)

1. To prepare the quince: preheat the oven to 350°F.

2. Add the lemon juice to a bowl with the water and then peel the quinces, saving the peelings. Quarter and core all the quince, discard the cores, and toss the quarters in the lemony water to prevent them from going brown.

3. Sprinkle the quince peel over the bottom of a small shallow baking dish or in a microwavable dish. Slice the quarters in half on top. Add the clementine zest and juice and then pour over the lemony water. Cover the dish snugly with a sheet of parchment, then foil (shiny side down to reflect the heat). Scrunch the foil tightly around the edges of the baking tray to prevent steam from escaping. If you are using a microwave, cover the bowl with plastic wrap.

(recipe continues)

4. Bake the quince in the oven for 2 hours. Otherwise you can microwave it on medium-high for 8 to 10 minutes, although a long, slow cooking is preferable. Remove from the oven and check the quince, which should be cooked to a coral-pink color and perfectly tender. Allow to cool, still covered with foil.

5. Once cold, transfer the quince pieces to a clean container and strain any remaining juice over the top, cover, and chill in the fridge (it will keep like this for about 5 days).

6. To prepare the ice cream: bring the milk and cream to a simmer in a non-reactive pan. Stir often, using a whisk or silicone spatula, to prevent it from catching. Once the liquid is hot and steaming, remove from the heat. Whisk the egg yolks, honey, and sugar together in a separate bowl until combined.

7. Pour the hot milk over the yolks in a thin stream, whisking continuously. Return all the mix to the pan and cook over low heat until it reaches 82°C/180°F. Stir constantly to avoid curdling the eggs and keep a close eye on it so as not to let it boil. As soon as your digital thermometer says 82°C/180°F, remove from the heat, then place the pan in a sink full of ice water to cool. Once the custard is at room temperature, cover with plastic wrap and chill in the fridge overnight.

8. To make the ice cream: the following day, scrape the quince and its juice into the custard, then blitz with an immersion blender until completely smooth, about 2 minutes. Use a small ladle to push the custard through a fine-mesh sieve or chinois to remove the grainy bits.

9. Pour the quince custard into an ice cream machine and churn according to the machine's instructions until frozen and the texture of whipped cream. The mixture is so thick it won't take long—15 to 20 minutes.

10. Transfer the ice cream to a suitable lidded container, sprinkling with frozen chunks of apple pie as you go (if using). Top with a piece of wax paper, cover, and freeze until ready to serve.

Note—This ice cream has a texture like thick, granular honey but the high amount of fiber in quince means that it freezes very hard. It needs a good 15 minutes in the fridge before it's soft enough to scoop.

# Pistachio Ice Creams

Pistachio nuts feel chic—when I was growing up in late-seventies England they were considered too expensive for children (fair enough), and the very few times I saw them at home the bowl was kept as far beyond reach as if they were green chips of jade.

Needless to say, these days I am hopelessly addicted. The shells, as pretty and as clattery as a plateful of clams, only serve as tiny obstacles to be overcome at speed, the aim being to cram as many nuts into my mouth as possible in a vain attempt to one day reach pistachio satisfaction. This compulsion must be what helps make pistachio ice cream so popular, both at home and abroad.

There will always be a place in my heart for the pistachio ice cream bought from Bar Italia in Soho—as green as their 1960s neon tube signage, with an intangible melon flavor and extra almond extract, served with a scoop of Tutti Frutti on the side.

A favorite afternoon delight is a cup of stretchy Syrian milk ice cream, or *éma'a*, from the sweet shop Damas Rose on the Edgware Road. The *éma'a* is pounded with pine-scented mastic (resin) and salep (orchid root) until thick and chewy. The ice cream is then smothered in a layer of chopped pistachio nuts before it's rolled up, sliced, and served with a flourish. Delicious and dense enough to last the walk down to catch a matinée at Curzon Mayfair.

Pistachio gelato gets better all the time, and you can recognize the quality by its dense matte texture and khaki color. My favorite version is from Gelateria da Ciccio (Fatty's) in Palermo, served in a fist-sized brioche. I had to fashion a bib from a pink sheet of *Gazzetto dello Sport* to stop it dripping over my lap. Pro tip: If you choose two or more flavors, a true *gelatiere* will always have been taught to make pistachio the smaller portion because it's so expensive. Beat the system and order a double scoop of the good stuff...

# PISTACHIO

The flavor you get from green-gold freshly roasted pistachios is incomparable—no paste or purée can better it no matter how fancy it might be. Timing is important; the hot toasted nuts should hiss as they hit the scalded milk and the vivid green oil is extracted from them—this way you ensure that all the flavor goes into your ice cream custard.

Best served for breakfast—slapped into a big squishy brioche and dipped in cappuccino.

100 g/4 oz raw shelled pistachio nuts
250 ml/1 cup whole milk
180 ml/¾ cup heavy cream
Generous pinch of sea salt
3 egg yolks
150 g/¾ cup sugar
1 teaspoon mild honey

1. To prepare the ice cream: preheat the oven to 350°F.

2. Toast the pistachios, spreading them out on a baking sheet in an even layer. Move them around every 4 or 5 minutes—you don't want them to color, only to crisp, but this could take up to 15 minutes so in the meantime you can start making the custard.

3. Heat the milk, cream, and salt together, stirring with a whisk or silicone spatula. When the liquid reaches a simmer, whisk the egg yolks, sugar, and honey together in a separate bowl until combined.

4. Pour the hot liquid over the yolks in a thin stream, whisking continuously. Return all the mix to the pan and cook over low heat until it reaches 82°C/180°F. Stir constantly to avoid curdling the eggs and keep a close eye on it so as not to let it boil. As soon as your digital thermometer says 82°C/180°F, remove the pan from the heat and set aside.

5. Take the toasted pistachio nuts from the oven and slide them, hot, directly into the hot custard. If you've timed it right the hot nuts should make a seething noise as they hit the custard. Pour this mixture into a food processor and liquidize for 2 to 3 minutes, watching the color slowly change to a vivid shade of green-gold. Scrape the custard into a clean container and place it in a sink of ice water to cool. Once the custard is at room temperature, cover tightly with plastic wrap and chill in the fridge.

6. To make the ice cream: the following day, remove the custard from the fridge. Liquidize it with an immersion blender and then pour into an ice cream machine. Churn according to the machine's instructions until frozen and the texture of whipped cream, 20 to 25 minutes.

7. Scrape the ice cream into a suitable lidded container. Top with a piece of wax paper to limit exposure to air, cover, and freeze until ready to serve.

Variations—You can substitute the pistachios for the same quantity of other kinds of nut with good results. Peanuts and blanched hazelnuts both make great alternatives. Pine nuts would be a luxurious choice. Walnuts are a favorite too, but keep a very close eye on them as they roast (the same goes for pine nuts). If they color anything beyond palest blond they will be too bitter to use in ice cream. Once you remove them from the oven, rub in a clean dish towel to remove the bitter skins before adding them to the custard.

# SATSUMA MIYAGAWA

Firm-fleshed, with poster-paint green peel and bright orange insides, satsuma Miyagawa are sharp, radiant, and full of fragrance. Like all green-skinned citrus fruit, they have highly aromatic zest, as seductive as a great aftershave. Make as much of it as you can—its oil makes all the difference in this sorbet.

Originally hailing from Japan but arriving in Europe and the United States via New Zealand, satsuma Miyagawa are the first citrus in the northern hemisphere to be ripe. Over a period of a few weeks its peel will begin to change from green to yellow, becoming baggy and less toothsome, so it's a good idea to seek out this citrus at the very beginning of the season.

I like to keep a few green fruits whole: slice off little "lids" and remove every drop of juice and pith before freezing the shells and refilling them with freshly churned sorbet. Replace the lids and hard freeze the whole lot. Serve wrapped in crinkly cellophane and tied with shiny ribbons for a retro dessert that has lost none of its power to impress.

I've always had a soft spot for lemon sorbet eaten out of its shell (*in guscio*) although you rarely see it in modern Italian restaurants. In Italy itself, I've only ever seen this dessert for sale in gas stations. Surprisingly, Italian gas (and railway) stations can often double up as quite good cafés—but are nonetheless odd places to find sorbet-stuffed frozen lemons.

This is also delicious served with Chocolate and Green Mandarin ice cream (page 205).

160 g/¾ cup sugar

160 ml/¾ cup water

8–12 satsuma Miyagawa (or use firm-fleshed clementines, satsuma, or mandarins)

1 lemon

1. To prepare the sorbet: heat the sugar and water together in a small non-reactive pan, stir to dissolve the sugar granules, and bring the syrup to a simmer. Remove from the heat.

2. Rinse and pat dry the citrus fruits. Zest the satsumas and the lemon directly into the pan of warm syrup, cover the pan with plastic wrap, and place in a sink full of ice water to cool.

3. Juice all of the citrus, and measure out 600 ml/2½ cups juice (drink any that is left over—yum!). Stir the juice into the cold syrup. Chill the mix for 2 to 3 hours in the fridge to chill thoroughly.

4. To make the sorbet: strain the liquid mix though a fine-mesh sieve or chinois and use a small ladle to squeeze the zest and extract as much juice and flavor from it as possible.

5. Pour the sorbet mix into an ice cream machine and churn according to the machine's instructions until frozen, thick, and snowy-looking, usually 20 to 25 minutes.

6. Transfer the sorbet to a suitable lidded container (or into the pre-frozen satsuma shells). Top with a piece of wax paper to limit exposure to air, cover, and freeze for at least 2 hours, or until ready to serve.

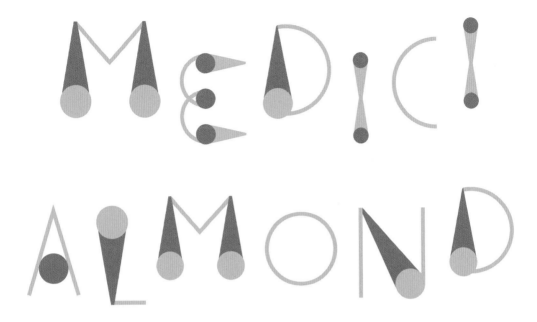

# MEDICI ALMOND

This is an exquisite almond sorbet flavored with spices popular in Renaissance Italy. I used to make it with raw almonds, ground and squeezed and pressed into milk. Now I've discovered there are really great quality almond butters available to buy that taste better, so I use them instead—saving myself a lot of washing up.

Look for white almond paste made from fatty and delicious Marcona almonds. Finely ground, this melts in your mouth in a silky, expensive way, rather than being too crunchy. It's worth seeking out an organic brand this time—only the organic trees still contain strains of wild almond, and these nuts in particular contribute the powerful and necessary bitter almond flavor.

If you prefer to keep things dairy-free, then this is super on its own, or try it with a shot of iced espresso poured over the top like the Pugliese drink *caffè in ghiacchio*. Otherwise, scoop this twinned with Mont-morency Cherry Sherbet (page 71) or topped with whipped cream and maraschino cherries, a scrap of gold leaf added for festivity.

Piece of cinnamon bark
1 bay leaf
5 black peppercorns
Dusting of nutmeg
Zest of ½ unwaxed lemon
150 g/¾ cup sugar
550 ml/2 cups water
1 tablespoon honey
150 g/⅔ cup organic white almond butter (I use the Biona brand)
2 drops of orange flower water

1. To prepare the sorbet: bash the spices and lemon zest in a mortar and pestle for a few seconds until lightly bruised.

2. Put the sugar, water, honey, and bruised spices into a pan and bring to a simmer, stirring until the sugar dissolves. As soon as the sugar syrup reaches the simmering point, remove it from the heat, add the almond butter and orange flower water, and whisk it in to incorporate, then place the pan in a sink full of ice water to cool. Cover and chill in the fridge for at least 4 hours or overnight.

3. To make the sorbet: the following day, whisk the almond syrup briskly, then strain the mix through a fine-mesh sieve or chinois, discarding the zest and spices.

4. Pour the sorbet mix into an ice cream machine and churn according to the machine's instructions until frozen, thick, and creamy-looking, usually 20 to 25 minutes.

5. Scrape the sorbet into a suitable lidded container. Top with a piece of wax paper to limit exposure to air, cover, and freeze for at least 2 hours, or until ready to serve. Best eaten within a week.

# ESPRESSO CON PANNA

Coffee ice cream is the greatest: one part of the holy trinity of flavors that used to make up my unbeatable regular order from the classic Giolitti caffè in Rome (the other two being zabaglione and pistachio, since you ask).

I've tried many different ways of making it, from experimenting with cold brew (so messy) to using shots of espresso (flavor gets lost) to sprinkling ground coffee in the mix (so grainy—don't do it). But the best results are achieved by this simple method of steeping good-quality, freshly roasted coffee beans in a custard base. You can control the desired strength by the length of time you steep the beans. My preference is for a bitter, strongly brewed frozen custard—pure heaven served in espresso cups with a spoonful of thick double cream on top.

300 ml/1¼ cups whole milk
300 ml/1¼ cups heavy cream
Pinch of sea salt
6 egg yolks
80 g/⅓ cup light brown muscovado sugar
20 g/2 tablespoons sugar
65 g/⅓ cup freshly roasted coffee beans
3 to 4 brown sugar cubes—the La Perruche brand is perfect and crunchy (optional)
1 tablespoon strong espresso, cooled (optional)

1. To prepare the ice cream: bring the milk, cream, and salt to a simmer in a non-reactive pan. Stir often, using a whisk or silicone spatula, to prevent it from catching. Once the liquid is hot and steaming, whisk the egg yolks and sugars together in a separate bowl until combined.

(recipe continues)

2. Pour the hot liquid over the yolks in a thin stream, whisking continuously. Return all the mix to the pan and cook over low heat until it reaches 82°C/180°F. Stir constantly to avoid curdling the eggs and keep a close eye on it so as not to let it boil. As soon as your digital thermometer says 82°C/180°F, remove the pan from the heat, add the coffee beans, and stir to submerge them in the custard. Cover the pan with plastic wrap and place in a sink full of ice water to cool. Set aside until cold, 30 to 40 minutes.

3. The longer you leave the beans in the custard, the stronger the flavor. Taste the custard: if once the mix has cooled the custard tastes like strong *café crème*, pass the mixture through a fine-mesh sieve or chinois, squeezing the beans to extract as much flavor as possible into the custard. Otherwise, chill the beans in the custard overnight and sieve the following day.

4. To make the ice cream: the following day, sieve the coffee beans, if you haven't already done so, and then liquidize the custard with an immersion blender for a minute until smooth.

5. Pour the custard into an ice cream machine and churn according to the machine's instructions until frozen and the texture of whipped cream, 20 to 25 minutes.

6. If using the sugar cubes, place them in a cup and pour the espresso over the top, allowing it to be absorbed by the sugar, then swirl the wet, treacly sugar into the churned ice cream.

7. Scrape the churned ice cream into a clean lidded container. Top with a piece of wax paper to limit exposure to air, cover, and freeze until ready to serve.

Note—Make sure the cream and milk you use are very fresh, otherwise there is a danger that the acidity of the coffee beans will curdle the mix. Leaving the coffee beans whole results in a white ice cream; roughly grinding them will turn the custard coffee colored.

# Chestnuts

About three weeks into my stay on the pig farm, on a day that Carlo was away, Gigia got a tip-off about some chestnut flour (i.e., perfect pig food) being given away by friends who lived on a farm in the Apennines, north of Modena. We bundled off in the car on a day trip, driving up higher and higher while the temperature dropped, until our breath fogged up the windshield. The "farm" was not much more than a wooden cabin divided into three rooms where a pair of ancient twin brothers lived and worked. A kitchen and a bedroom formed the ground floor; the attic space with its slatted floorboards was reserved for drying the sweet chestnuts they harvested above a big wood fire in an adjacent lean-to.

The brothers welcomed us after our long drive with lunch cooked on a 1970s range stove of great charm in an otherwise empty room, bar clean linoleum floor, table, and four chairs. We drank dark, fizzy chestnut beer and ate nubbins of peppery salami, followed by plates of fine eggy homemade chestnut tagliatelle and wild boar ragù and finally the obligatory espresso and a smoky square of deeply savory *castagnaccio* (most probably baked in *strutto*, or pork fat) and scattered with pine nuts, rosemary, and raisins. The ingredients used to cook the entire meal can't have numbered more than half a dozen.

I dream of reproducing that lunch—right down to the floor, the fairy tale brothers, and the flavors that reminded me of the smell from those misty hills and surrounding woods. We drove home with half a dozen 25 kg/50 lb bags of free chestnut flour for the pigs. The brothers had been persuaded to pack the flour in plastic sacks for the first time after many years of previously having used hessian, and their annual harvest had gone rancid. Simple and good wins every time for me.

# ROAST CHESTNUT CREMOLATA

This is a simple, nourishing ice of few ingredients. Whole milk enriched with roasted chestnuts and sugar creates a light texture and subtle woody flavor. *Cremolate* is the name given in Italy to eggless ices that are only partly frozen. Softer and less icy than granita, the flavor is bright and very pure, but they are best eaten straightaway.

Because it is so simple it's worth using the grassiest, creamiest milk you can afford. Roasting the chestnuts either on a wood fire or coals will make the ice cream taste smoky. Otherwise, here's a secret: you can save yourself the time it takes to peel 400 g/1 lb chestnuts (a long time) and use unsweetened chestnut purée instead—and it's still delicious. Serve with whipped cream laced with rum and vanilla.

400 g/1 lb fresh whole chestnuts (or 220 g/8 oz unsweetened chestnut purée)
500 ml/2 cups whole milk
170 g/¾ cup + 1 tablespoon sugar
1 vanilla pod, split
Pinch of sea salt
50 g/¼ cup dark chocolate, grated

(recipe continues)

187

1. To prepare the cremolata: preheat the oven to 400°F.

2. Using a small, sharp knife, score a long cross through the skin of each chestnut. Take care to do this properly, as it will make the nuts easier to peel once they are roasted. Roast them on a baking sheet for 30 minutes.

3. Warm the milk, sugar, vanilla, and salt in a medium pan or in the microwave, stirring to dissolve the sugar. When the milk is steaming and the sugar has dissolved, remove it from the heat and set aside.

4. Remove the chestnuts from the oven and peel them while they're hot. Use a dish towel to hold them and wear rubber gloves if necessary. Weigh out 220 g/8 oz of the peeled chestnuts (or unsweetened chestnut purée) and add this to the warm milk. Liquidize for 2 minutes until perfectly smooth, and then use a small ladle to pass the mixture through a fine-mesh sieve or chinois to remove any bits of skin and the vanilla pod.

5. Pour the chestnut milk into a clean container, then place this in a sink of ice water to cool. As soon as it reaches room temperature, cover and chill in the fridge.

6. To make the cremolata: the following day, liquidize the cremolata with an immersion blender for 1 minute to emulsify completely.

7. Pour the mix into an ice cream machine and churn according to the machine's instructions until frozen and the texture of whipped cream, 20 to 25 minutes.

8. Transfer the cremolata into a suitable lidded container, sprinkling it with grated chocolate as you go. Top with a piece of wax paper to limit exposure to air, cover, and freeze, ideally for just an hour before serving. Best eaten the same day.

# BUTTERSCOTCH AND AGEN PRUNE

Grassy, salted Breton butter, burnt sugar, and prunes—stirring these good things up together makes one *delicieux* ice cream. Prune haters (if you are friends with any) need never know they are contained within. Their addition just adds a fruity toffee depth to the custard which, once churned, is rippled with a salty butterscotch sauce. Adding butter to an ice cream base increases the amount of protein, creating body and slight chewiness (it's how the delicious Scottish version of *fiore di latte*—brilliantly called "white" ice cream—is made).

*For the butterscotch ripple* (makes more than you need)
200 g/1 cup sugar
85 g/¾ stick (6 tablespoons) unsalted butter
120 ml/½ cup heavy cream, at room temperature
1½ teaspoons fine sea salt (*sel de Guérande*)

*For the ice cream*
20 g/2 tablespoons salted Brittany butter
100 g/½ cup soft light brown sugar
300 ml/1¼ cups heavy cream
1 teaspoon vanilla extract
240 ml/1 cup whole milk
5 egg yolks
60 g (about 4) Agen prunes (stone in weight), pitted and chopped

1. To make the butterscotch: sprinkle the bottom of a heavy-based pan (ideally stainless steel) with an even layer of the sugar. Place it over medium heat and cook slowly (not stirring) until it begins to melt and caramelize. Swirl the pan for even caramelization. If it starts crystallizing into sugary chunks, turn the heat right down and wait. The sugar will eventually melt and get darker and darker in color.

2. Cook the caramel to a rich amber color, then whisk in the butter until melted and combined. Remove from the heat and whisk in the cream and sea salt. It will bubble up, so be careful. Whisk vigorously until all the cream is incorporated into a smooth caramel sauce.

3. Set the pan aside and allow to cool before pouring half of the butterscotch into a thick plastic piping bag. Fasten the wide end shut with a clip or tight knot. Save the extra butterscotch in a clean lidded jar. It will keep in the fridge for up to 2 weeks.

4. To prepare the ice cream: melt the butter in a small sturdy pan over low heat. Stir in half the brown sugar until it's wet. Stir every so often until it looks like molten lava. It will take about 5 minutes.

5. Watch closely as the mixture starts to caramelize: the brown sugar will begin to look and feel more like liquid and less like thick wet sand. At this point, whisk in the cream and vanilla, turn the heat to medium so that the mixture cooks at a controlled simmer, and whisk every few minutes for a total of 10 minutes.

6. Add the milk and whisk in to combine. Mix the egg yolks and remaining brown sugar in a bowl, then pour the warm liquid over in a thin stream, whisking continuously. Return the mix to the pan and cook over low heat until it reaches 82°C/180°F, stirring all the time to avoid curdling, and making sure it doesn't boil. As soon as your digital thermometer says 82°C/180°F, remove the pan from the heat, add the chopped prunes and stir them in, then place the pan into a sink of ice water to cool. Speed up the cooling process by stirring the mix every so often. Once the custard is at room temperature, scrape it into a clean container, cover with plastic wrap, and chill.

7. To make the ice cream: the following day, liquidize the cold custard until as smooth as possible, 2 to 3 minutes. Pour the custard through a fine-mesh sieve or chinois into a clean container.

8. Pour the custard into an ice cream machine and churn according to the machine's instructions until frozen and the texture of whipped cream, 20 to 25 minutes.

9. Snip the tip off the piping bag of butterscotch. Transfer the ice cream into a suitable lidded container, piping thick squiggles of butterscotch over the ice cream as you go. Top with a piece of wax paper to limit exposure to air, cover, and freeze until ready to serve.

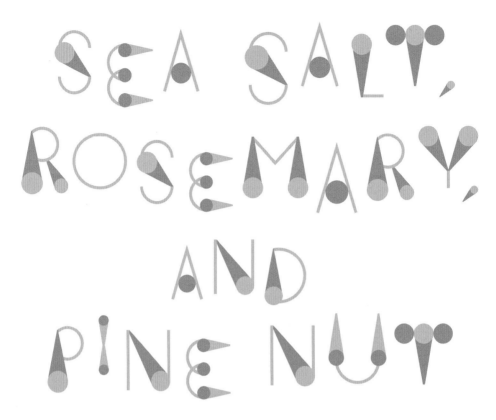

# SEA SALT, ROSEMARY, AND PINE NUT

Sadly, I can't make this ice cream that often because it annoys me too much the way people see the words "sea salt" and literally screech to a halt in front of my ice cream van when it's on the menu. What is it with sea salt? Sprinkle it on strawberry yogurt if you love it that much—I'll be just fine here with all the fresh peach ice cream that no one pays any attention to. Pine nuts, though, I can get excited about. I've joined Facebook groups for them! Fatty and addictive, they have a smokiness that pairs well with sweet and savory flavors. In this recipe, liberally salted pine nut brittle is stirred into rosemary-scented caramel custard ice cream and it's utterly delicious. Try it served alongside Roast Chestnut Cremolata (page 187).

*For the pine nut and rosemary brittle*
100 g/4 oz pine nuts
100 g/¾ cup sugar
1 heaping teaspoon glucose syrup (makes caramel easier to manage)
20 g/2 tablespoons butter
15 g/1 oz rosemary leaves
¼ teaspoon baking powder
1 teaspoon sea salt

(recipe continues)

*For the ice cream*
120 g/⅔ cup sugar
300 ml/1¼ cups heavy cream
300 ml/1¼ cups whole milk
Pinch of sea salt
6 egg yolks
20 to 25 fresh rosemary leaves

1. To make the pine nut and rosemary brittle: toast the pine nuts over very low heat in a pan for 10 minutes, until warmed and just colored, then pour them into a bowl and cover with a clean dish towel to keep them warm.

2. Heat the sugar, glucose, and a tablespoon of water together slowly in a pan until the grains of sugar have dissolved. Swirl the pan to mix; do not stir. Add the butter, bring the mix to a boil, and boil steadily until it reaches 150°C/300°F on your digital thermometer.

3. Meanwhile, pick the rosemary leaves, adding them to the bowl of pine nuts along with the baking powder and sea salt, then mix well, ensuring there are no lumps of baking powder. Have a whisk or heat-proof spatula at hand.

4. As soon as the sugar reaches 150°C/300°F, or a dark caramel color, tip in the pine nut mix and whisk well to combine. The mixture will bubble up because of the baking powder, so use a long heatproof spatula or whisk to keep your hands safe from burns. Allow the rosemary to sizzle and the nuts to toast to a pale gold color in the caramel, then remove from the heat.

5. Pour the hot brittle evenly onto a silicone baking mat. Cover with another non-stick baking mat or a double sheet of buttered parchment, and roll quickly and firmly with a wooden rolling pin to evenly spread the brittle into a half-centimeter layer. Leave to cool.

6. Break the brittle into large pieces and store between sheets of wax paper in an airtight container, or roughly smash into chunks ready to add to the freshly churned rosemary-caramel ice cream.

7. To prepare the ice cream: sprinkle the bottom of a heavy-based pan (ideally stainless steel) with 100 g/½ cup of the sugar in an even layer. Place it over medium heat and cook slowly and without stirring

until it begins to melt and caramelize. Swirl the pan to achieve even caramelization.

8. Cook the caramel to a dark color until just smoking, then pour in the cream and milk to stop the cooking process. Add the sea salt and warm the liquids over a medium heat to dissolve the caramel; this may take 10 minutes. Stir, but do not boil, as you don't want to evaporate the liquid too much. Once the caramel has dissolved, whisk the remaining 20 g/2 tablespoons sugar with the egg yolks until combined.

9. Pour the hot liquid over the yolks in a thin stream, whisking continuously. Return all the mix to the pan and cook over a low heat until it reaches 82°C/180°F, stirring all the time to avoid curdling the eggs and keeping a close eye on it so as not to let it boil. As soon as your digital thermometer says 82°C/180°F, remove from the heat, add the fresh rosemary leaves and stir them in, then place the pan in a sink of ice water to cool. Speed up the cooling process by stirring the mix every so often. Once the custard is at room temperature, transfer it into a clean container, cover with plastic wrap, and chill.

10. To make the ice cream: the following day, use a small ladle to push the custard through a fine-mesh sieve or chinois into a clean container. Discard the rosemary leaves, then liquidize the cold custard with an immersion blender, about 1 minute.

11. Pour the custard into an ice cream machine and churn according to the machine's instructions, until frozen and the texture of whipped cream, 20 to 25 minutes.

12. Transfer the ice cream to a suitable lidded container, sprinkling in generous handfuls of crushed pine nut brittle as you go (you will need about half the amount you made). Top with a piece of wax paper to limit exposure to air, cover, and freeze until ready to serve.

Note—You can store any extra brittle between sheets of wax paper in an airtight container. I always save silica gel sachets and slip one of these in too for good measure (to help keep the brittle crisp).

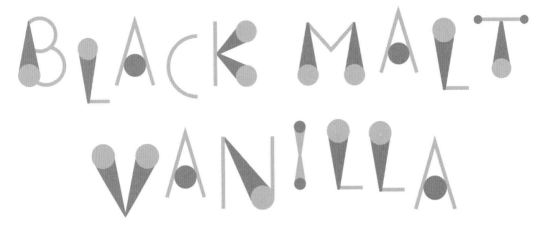

# BLACK MALT VANILLA

Black malt is the name given to roasted grains of malted barley—traditionally the grain used in the brewing industry to make porter (and, as a consequence, easily available online for the home brewing crew). Steeped overnight in an egg custard base, it produces a creamy, biscuit-colored ice cream with rich complex toasted coffee and nut flavors, which are enhanced by thick malt syrup and vanilla bean. It's a real spoon-licker. Serve with Banana, Brown Sugar, and Rum ice cream (page 54), if you like.

1 vanilla pod
220 ml/1 cup whole milk
300 ml/1¼ cups heavy cream
Pinch of sea salt
5 egg yolks
45 g/¼ cup sugar
40 g/¼ cup light brown muscovado sugar
20 g/1 tablespoon malt extract
30 g/2 tablespoons black malt

1. To prepare the ice cream: split the vanilla pod lengthwise and scrape out the seeds, adding both the seeds and pod to a non-reactive pan along with the milk, cream, and salt. Bring the mixture to a simmer, stirring often, using a whisk or silicone spatula, to prevent it catching. Once the liquid is hot and steaming, whisk the egg yolks, sugars, and malt extract together in a separate bowl until combined.

(recipe continues)

2. Pour the hot liquid over the egg mix in a thin stream, whisking continuously. Return all the mix to the pan and cook over low heat until it reaches 82°C/180°F. Stir constantly to avoid curdling the eggs and keep a close eye on it so as not to let it boil. As soon as your digital thermometer says 82°C/180°F, remove from the heat and stir the grains of black malt into the custard. Place the pan in a sink full of ice water to cool, stirring the mix occasionally to speed up the cooling process. Once cold, cover with plastic wrap, and chill in the fridge.

3. To make the ice cream: the following day, use a small ladle to push the custard through a fine-mesh sieve or chinois. Squeeze hard to extract as much toffee-colored custard from the malt as possible. Discard the malt and keep the vanilla pod to rinse and dry later (see page 19), then liquidize the custard with an immersion blender until smooth, about 1 minute.

4. Pour the custard into an ice cream machine and churn according to the machine's instructions until frozen and the texture of whipped cream, 20 to 25 minutes.

5. Transfer the churned ice cream to a clean lidded container. Top with a piece of wax paper to limit exposure to air, cover, and freeze until ready to serve.

# Chocolate Ice Creams

It can be useful sometimes to understand the chemistry behind a recipe to see what makes it work.

The difficulty in making chocolate ice cream is that natural vegetable fats (the fats contained in the cocoa butter within the chocolate) freeze hard—much harder than the animal fats (in cream and egg yolks) that are usually present in ice cream. This can make homemade chocolate ice cream hard to scoop, and dry and chalky once frozen.

The first way to remedy this is to use a good-quality cocoa powder instead of real chocolate. It might seem counterintuitive (surely using real chocolate gives a better-tasting result?), but in fact using chocolate adds cocoa butter and sugar to your base, both of which mute the intense chocolate flavor once mixed with the other ingredients. Using a good-quality cocoa will give you all the rich flavor without upsetting the balance of your recipe.

Another trick is to caramelize the sugar. Caramelizing sugar changes its composition, making it act a bit like glucose syrup and making the ice cream much softer to scoop, while also adding depth of flavor and a touch of bitterness. A generous pinch of sea salt will balance things nicely.

# CHOCOLATE CARAMEL

Velvety chocolate pudding–flavored ice cream. Eat this with a friend so she can wrestle the tub from you before you polish it off in one go.

Cooking the cocoa out properly in the milk is really important so it ends up silky rather than chalky and doesn't have that raw taste. Don't skimp on this step—it needs 6 full minutes of simmering. A sprinkle of grated chocolate in the freshly churned ice cream at the end makes every mouthful of this feel slightly different, thus keeping your tongue interested.

350 ml/1½ cups whole milk
30 g/⅓ cup best possible cocoa powder
250 ml/1 cup heavy cream
Pinch of sea salt
150 g/¾ cup sugar
4 egg yolks
1 tablespoon golden syrup or malt syrup
30 g/1 oz chocolate, grated or cocoa nibs

1. To prepare the ice cream: pour a little of the cold milk into the cocoa powder, stir to make a paste, and whisk in the rest of the milk. Add the milk to a pan and bring to a boil, stirring constantly, then simmer gently for exactly 6 minutes. Keep stirring, as the cocoa can easily burn, then after 6 minutes whisk in the cream and salt.

2. Sprinkle the sugar in an even layer into a non-stick frying pan or non-reactive pan. Heat until melted, swirling the pan occasionally, and caramelize until the color of a horse chestnut and just beginning to smoke. Stop the caramelization at this point by pouring the caramel into the chocolate milk (take care, as it will bubble and sputter). Whisk or stir over low heat until all the caramel is dissolved in the milk. In a separate bowl, whisk the egg yolks with a little of the warm chocolate milk and the golden syrup until combined.

3. Pour the rest of the hot chocolate liquid over the yolks in a thin stream, whisking continuously. Return all the mix to the pan and cook over low heat until it reaches 82°C/180°F. Stir constantly to avoid curdling the eggs and keep a close eye on it so as not to let it boil. As soon as your digital thermometer says 82°C/180°F, remove from the heat, then place the pan in a sink full of ice water to cool. Set aside until cold, about 30 minutes. Once the custard is cold, pour into a clean container, cover with plastic wrap, and chill in the fridge overnight.

4. To make the ice cream: the following day, liquidize the chocolate custard with an immersion blender until smooth.

5. Pour the custard into an ice cream machine and churn according to the instructions or until frozen and the texture of whipped cream. The mixture is so thick it shouldn't take long—15 to 20 minutes.

6. Scrape the ice cream into a suitable lidded container. Sprinkle in the grated chocolate as you go. Top with a piece of wax paper to limit exposure to air, cover, and freeze until ready to serve.

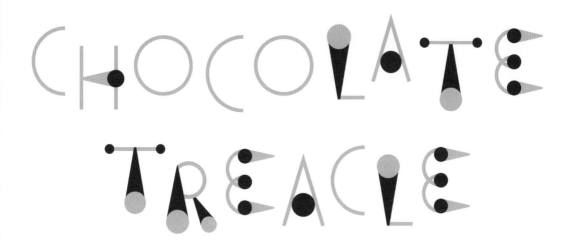

# CHOCOLATE TREACLE

A deep, dark, delicious variation on the Chocolate Caramel ice cream recipe (page 200). Treacle toffee (known in Olde Worlde Englande as Bonfire Toffee) is frozen and smashed into pieces before being added to the churned ice cream. These dark, glassy shards will eventually melt into sticky molasses nuggets. Beware of flying shards of frozen toffee when you make this, which will embed themselves in hair and sweaters and mysteriously spread to all corners of the kitchen floor and walls—you will still be finding bits weeks later. In other words, the gift that keeps on giving!

*For the treacle toffee* (makes more than you need)
450 g/2 cups light brown muscovado sugar
125 g/½ cup hot water
115 g/⅓ cup black treacle or molasses
115 g/⅓ cup golden syrup
1 teaspoon white wine vinegar
75 g/5 tablespoons unsalted butter

*For the ice cream*
350 ml/1½ cups whole milk
30 g/⅓ cup best possible cocoa powder
250 ml/1 cup heavy cream
Pinch of sea salt
140 g/⅔ cup sugar
4 egg yolks
1 teaspoon black treacle or molasses

(recipe continues)

1. To make the treacle toffee: butter then line a 20 × 30 cm/8 x 12 inch baking sheet with parchment.

2. Measure all the ingredients into a deep, heavy-based pan. Place over medium heat and stir occasionally until the butter is melted and the sugar has dissolved. When the mixture is smooth and well combined, increase the heat and bring the mixture to a really fast boil. Cook until the mixture reaches 140°C/275°F, about 30 minutes, then pour the mixture carefully into the lined baking sheet.

3. Let the toffee cool completely, then break into large pieces with a toffee hammer (toffee-hammer!) or rolling pin. Freeze the toffee first if necessary.

4. Place a large piece of toffee weighing about 40 g/2 oz into a sturdy zip-top bag in the freezer. Keep frozen until ready to use. Once your ice cream is churned, smash the toffee into small shards using a rolling pin. Store the rest in an airtight container, with individual layers of toffee separated by parchment. If left exposed to humidity, the toffee will soften and stick together.

5. To prepare the ice cream: pour a little of the cold milk into the cocoa powder, stir to make a paste, then whisk in the rest of the milk. Add the milk to a pan and bring to a boil, stirring constantly, then simmer gently for exactly 6 minutes. It is really important to cook out the cocoa so it ends up silky rather than chalky. Stir or whisk constantly, as the cocoa burns easily (a heart-spring whisk is really useful for this), then after 6 minutes whisk in the cream and salt.

6. Sprinkle the sugar in an even layer into a non-stick frying pan or non-reactive pan. Heat until melted, swirling the pan occasionally, and caramelize until the color of a horse chestnut. Stop the caramelization by pouring the caramel into the chocolate milk. Whisk or stir over low heat until all the caramel is dissolved in the milk (this may take a few minutes). In a separate bowl, whisk the egg yolks with a little of the warm chocolate milk and the black treacle until combined.

7. Pour the rest of the hot chocolate liquid over the yolks in a thin stream, whisking continuously. Return all the mix to the pan and cook over low heat until it reaches 82°C/180°F. Stir constantly to avoid curdling the eggs and keep a close eye on it so as not to let it boil. As soon as your digital thermometer says 82°C/180°F, remove

from the heat, then place the pan in a sink full of ice water to cool. Set aside until room temperature, about 30 minutes. Once the custard is at room temperature, pour into a clean container, cover with plastic wrap, and chill in the fridge overnight.

8. To make the ice cream: the following day, liquidize the chocolate custard with an immersion blender until smooth.

9. Pour the custard into an ice cream machine and churn according to the instructions or until frozen and the texture of whipped cream— the mixture is thick, so it shouldn't take long, 15 to 20 minutes.

10. Scrape the ice cream into a suitable lidded container, sprinkling in the smashed treacle toffee as you go. Top with a piece of wax paper to limit exposure to air, cover, and freeze until ready to serve.

Variations—For a Chocolate and Green Mandarin ice cream, follow the recipe above but caramelize the sugar to a lighter amber color, then "stop" it by whisking it into the chocolate milk. Once the custard is completely cool, use a microplane to grate in the zest of three green mandarins (or use one fragrant orange or any of your favorite citrus fruit). Whisk the zest into the custard, cover, and chill overnight. The following day, strain the custard through a fine-mesh sieve or chinois to remove the zest before churning.

To make Chocolate Ristretto ice cream, add a tablespoon of very strong hot espresso and a heaping teaspoon of soft light brown sugar to a bowl and stir until the sugar dissolves. Leave to cool. Whisk the cold, sweet *ristretto* into the chocolate custard before churning.

For a Chocolate and Caper ice cream, follow the recipe above but caramelize the sugar to a lighter amber color, then "stop" it by whisking in the cream and salt (omit the sea salt from the recipe). Soak 1 tablespoon of salted capers (not the brined ones!) in 500 ml/2 cups warm water for half an hour. Remove the capers from the water and squeeze them very dry in your fingers. Blend the capers into the cold custard for a couple of minutes before churning, for a salty tang.

# LEAFY CLEMENTINE GRANITA

Before I moved to New York I had no idea anywhere could be that hot. It was exciting—stepping out of an air-conditioned building and into the street had a kind of sink-or-swim feel about it and you just had to dive in. But it was also disgusting—I had no air conditioning in my tiny studio apartment and it was there that I discovered that sweat has a color.

Working in the kitchen of a pizza restaurant was almost worse; I would come up from a trip to the sweltering basement changing rooms looking like I was fresh out of the shower, hair plastered to my head like a hot-faced baby.

But it's in temperatures like this that granita really comes into its own. We usually had a couple of different fresh fruit flavors on the go in the kitchen, spinning away in big slushed ice machines looked after by the Sri Lankan bar-back Dinesh. At 5 p.m., when my shift was over, he would let me fill a 16-ounce wax paper cup with a mixture of fragrant lemon and tangerine granita, crushed ice, and soda water. Sipped slowly through a straw, this lasted just long enough to see me home along baking concrete sidewalks.

This clementine granita has a soft citrus flavor like a summertime glass of orange squash, but is given bite with the addition of its own dark, spicy perfumed leaves.

2 kg/4 lb leafy clementines (about 20)
90 g/½ cup sugar
40 ml/¼ cup water
1 lemon

1. Place a large, shallow stainless steel baking sheet or dish in the freezer to get very cold.

2. Rinse the clementines and any leaves, then pat them dry with paper towels (it's impossible to zest them otherwise).

3. Heat the sugar, water, and clementine leaves together in a small pan, stirring until the grains of sugar have dissolved and the syrup starts to simmer. Remove the syrup from the heat. Using a microplane (rather than a cheese grater, which would bite through the pith), zest half of the clementines directly into the hot syrup, then set this aside to cool.

4. Juice all of the clementines and the lemon, then measure out 550 ml/2 cups juice and add this to the cold syrup. Use a small ladle to push this liquid through a fine-mesh sieve or chinois to remove the leaves, zest, and any seeds. Squeeze hard to extract as much flavor from them as possible.

5. Pour the liquid into the frozen sheet and return it to the freezer, carefully placing it flat upon a shelf. Once an hour has passed, check the granita; it should have begun to freeze around the edges. Use a fork to break up any frozen bits and stir them back into the mix.

6. Every 45 minutes, return to stir the granita. Keep agitating it to prevent it from freezing solid. The aim is to achieve large, slushy frozen crystals.

7. The end result after about 3 hours should be a heap of sparkling ice crystals. Serve in chilled glasses with softly whipped cream. This can be kept covered in the freezer for up to a week, but you'll need to scrape it with a fork before serving to break up any large lumps.

Note—If you can't find clementines with leaves attached use fresh kaffir lime leaves instead, or go without for a simpler tasting but ultimately equally refreshing granita. You could also substitute the clementines for tangerines, satsumas, or blood oranges, if you prefer.

# Looking for a Date

Date shakes are a specialty of Palm Springs, California, and are made from a mixture of sticky dates, cold fresh milk, vanilla ice cream, and crushed ice. These ingredients are blended until frothy, dusted with nutmeg, and served from road stands, perfect alongside a piece of pineapple upside-down cake and perhaps a handful of tangerines.

They are one of those must-do foods that make perfect sense in the place they are being eaten—like drinking from a cool green coconut on the beach in Brazil or… um… eating a crunchy apple in England in the autumn. (Why hasn't anyone started a "street food" company of refrigerated apple carts here in London—not exciting enough?).

In fact, when I went to California with my husband, John, and 6-month-old baby, Jean, to make my highly anticipated road trip along route 111, we managed to pass by every date shake stand. After U-turns in the dust, and driving back and forth over the same bit of highway, GPS swirling, Johnny had had enough and I never got my date shake.

So, until we can get back to Shields Date Gardens, I order a big box of Palm Springs dates every year and make Date Shake ice cream. Medjool and Deglet Noor dates have a natural caramel flavor and are so sweet that you barely need to add any extra sugar, and the added fiber from the dates makes the ice cream extra rich and thick.

I also make a Date & Espresso ice cream that takes its inspiration from the Egyptian café in the Piazza della Madonna in Monti in Rome, where I ordered coffee and date ice cream, really wanting it to be delicious. It wasn't—much too sweet—but my recipe is! To adjust the opposite recipe, just add 2 tablespoons of hot, strong ristretto and 2 teaspoons of soft light brown sugar to a bowl and stir until the sugar dissolves, then leave to cool. Whisk the cold, sweet espresso into the date and vanilla custard just before churning.

# DATE SHAKE

Serve this with Novellino Orange Jelly (page 28), Espresso con Panna ice cream (page 183), or a slice of pineapple upside-down cake, if you know what's good for you.

225 ml/1 cup whole milk
225 ml/1 cup heavy cream
1 vanilla pod, split lengthwise
Pinch of sea salt
Dusting of freshly grated nutmeg
3 large egg yolks
50 g/⅓ cup sugar
60 g/2 oz Medjool dates, pitted

1. To prepare the ice cream: bring the milk, cream, split vanilla pod, salt, and nutmeg to a simmer in a non-reactive pan. Stir often to prevent it from catching. Once the liquid is hot and steaming, whisk the egg yolks and sugar together in a separate bowl until combined.

2. Pour the hot milk over the yolks in a thin stream, whisking continuously. Return all the mix to the pan and cook over low heat until it reaches 82°C/180°F. Stir constantly to avoid curdling and make sure it doesn't boil. As soon as your digital thermometer says 82°C/180°F, remove from the heat and stir the dates into the custard. Place the pan in a sink full of ice water to cool, stirring the mix occasionally. Once cold, cover with plastic wrap and chill in the fridge.

3. To make the ice cream: the following day, pick out the vanilla pod from the custard, squeeze out the seeds, and add these to the custard. Liquidize the custard and dates together with an immersion blender until very smooth, about 2 minutes. Use a small ladle to push the custard through a fine-mesh sieve or chinois, removing any lumps.

4. Pour the custard into an ice cream machine and churn according to the machine's instructions until frozen and the texture of whipped cream, 20 to 25 minutes.

5. Scrape the churned ice cream into a clean lidded container. Top with a piece of wax paper, cover, and freeze until ready to serve.

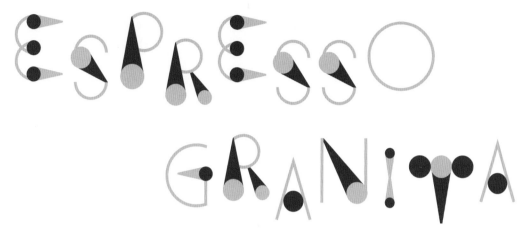

ESPRESSO GRANITA

Working the evening shift in the kitchens of the American Academy in Rome meant I could spend my mornings down the hill in Bar San Calisto. Here, as well as great coffee and dizzyingly strong *sgroppino*, you could buy paper cups of homemade espresso or lemon granita for a euro a pop. If you nodded yes to the question *"Vuoi panna?"* the granita would come enveloped in a kind of puffer jacket of whipped cream. Apart from being completely delicious, and tempering the bitterness of the syrupy black slush, this worked like insulation on the granita, preventing it from melting too quickly as I sat reading old copies of *The New Yorker* and watching the world go by on the Piazza di Santa Maria in Trastevere.

I've tried to nail this recipe, but encourage you to take a relaxed view toward any discrepancies given that it's difficult to define "strong coffee." People have different ideas about how strong "strong" is and the different ways of making espresso—unless you are a barista it might taste different every time. Taste the unfrozen mixture first—it should be bracingly sweet and strong but not unpleasantly bitter. If you want to add a little extra water or sugar or coffee, go right ahead, just don't veer too far from the original.

130 g/¾ cup sugar
130 ml/½ cup water
1 Amalfi or unwaxed lemon (optional)
490 ml/2 cups freshly brewed espresso (about 8 double shots) or very strong coffee
1 tablespoon nocino, grappa, or anisette liqueur (optional)

(recipe continues)

1. Place a large shallow stainless steel baking sheet or dish in the freezer to get very cold.

2. Heat the sugar, water, and a couple of strips of lemon zest (if using) together in a small pan, stirring until the grains of sugar have dissolved and the syrup starts to simmer. Remove the syrup from the heat.

3. Add the coffee to the syrup, remove any pieces of zest, and stir in the *ammazzacaffè* (translates as "coffee-killing") liqueur if you like the flavor. Leave the liquid to cool in a sink full of ice water.

4. Once cold, pour the liquid into the frozen tray and return it to the freezer, carefully placing it flat on a shelf. After an hour has passed, check the granita; it should have begun to freeze around the edges. Use a fork to break up any frozen bits and stir them back into the mix.

5. Every 45 minutes, return to stir the granita. Keep agitating it to prevent it from freezing solid. The aim is large, slushy frozen crystals.

6. The end result after about 3 hours should be a heap of tobacco-colored ice crystals. Serve in chilled glasses with softly whipped cream. This can be kept covered in the freezer for up to one week, but you'll need to scrape it with a fork before serving to break up any large lumps.

# RICOTTA AND CANDITI

Hidden within the Sunday morning wasteland of Naples' commercial ferry port lies a local secret...

If you weave your way in past the empty shipping containers and manage to locate it you might be surprised to find a tiny *pasticceria*, brimming with shouty Neapolitans, anxious to possess the heavily laden boxes of Sicilian pastries—fresh off the boat from Palermo that morning—to bring to Sunday lunch.

I would buy a carefully wrapped gold cardboard tray of *cannoli* and *cassata* (truly wonderful words) and wander up the hill toward Palazzo Reale to find an espresso bar to sit outside. Here I could watch the boats chugging off toward Capri while sinking my teeth through the various delights of thick green marzipan, *pan di spagna*, wobbly sheep's milk ricotta, and golden cannolo shells, the authentic ones having the crunch that only something fried in lard can lay claim to.

This ice cream reminds me of all of those good things. The salinity and slightly grainy texture of the ricotta ice cream provides a cool background for the rich mixture of bitter chocolate chips, pistachio nuts, and luminous candied citrus peel.

200 g/1 cup buffalo or sheep's milk ricotta
15 g/1 tablespoon tapioca starch (or use cornstarch)
120 g/⅔ cup sugar
400 ml/1½ cups whole milk
1 tablespoon dry Marsala wine
1 teaspoon mild honey
2 teaspoons orange flower water
Pinch of ground espresso
25 g/1 oz chopped candied citrus peel
25 g/1 oz chopped dark chocolate
25 g/1 oz chopped lightly toasted pistachio nuts

1. To prepare the ice cream: set the ricotta to drain in a sieve over a bowl. Meanwhile, whisk the tapioca starch or cornstarch and sugar together in a bowl.

(recipe continues)

2. Heat the milk to the simmering point, then pour it in a thin stream over the tapioca, whisking constantly to prevent lumps forming. Return this mix to the pan, and bring it back to a simmer to cook out the starch. Whisk constantly, as it can catch and burn easily at this point.

3. Remove from the heat, then whisk the ricotta, Marsala, and honey into the milk before placing the pan in a sink of ice water to cool. Speed up the cooling process by stirring the mixture every so often. Once the custard is at room temperature, stir in the orange flower water, cover with plastic wrap, and chill in the fridge overnight.

4. Mix the espresso, chopped peel, chocolate, and toasted nuts together and place in the freezer in a lidded container (this is so that they won't melt the ice cream once they are added to it).

5. To make the ice cream: remove the custard from the fridge and blend it well for about a minute to re-liquefy the mix and make it easier to pour into the ice cream machine.

6. Pour the mix into an ice cream machine and churn according to the machine's instructions until frozen and the texture of softly whipped cream, 20 to 25 minutes.

7. Transfer the ice cream to a suitable lidded container, sprinkling with the frozen "canditi" as you go until they are used up. Top with a piece of wax paper to limit exposure to air, cover, and freeze until ready to serve.

Note—This is a milk-based ice with no eggs to better allow the delicate flavor of the ricotta to shine. The tapioca starch thickens and some-what emulsifies the ice cream base. Tapioca looks gloopy but I like the chewy effect it has on the base—otherwise cornstarch works simi-larly. This ice cream will freeze hard because of the starch, so remove it a good 10 minutes before you want to serve it.

Variation—To make Ricotta and Maraschino Cherry ice cream, make up a batch of the ricotta ice cream but substitute the orange flower water with a teaspoon of vanilla extract. Once churned, stir in mara-schino cherries and a little of their syrup before hard freezing.

# LIME AND BOTANICALS

This sorbet has all the twinkle and fresh, green vim of a top-shelf gin and tonic, only it's better as it doesn't contain any booze. Alcohol affects the texture of sorbet—lowering the freezing temperature and making it sloppy textured. Excellent for *sgroppino* (aka alcoholic slush puppy), but that is not always what you want.

This sorbet is uplifting: the smell of lime zest, along with simmering botanicals—juniper, angelica, coriander, and cinnamon—fills the kitchen with fresh herbaceous essences. You can't help but suddenly feel more positive about the immediate future as you make it.

Juicing limes can feel less uplifting, especially if you've bought the hard, unyielding kind—so select thin-skinned, juicy ones. In any case, your labors will be worth it for this refreshing and festive sorbet. This makes a favorite non-alcoholic drink served in a tall glass with bubbly soda water and extra ice, particularly if you can find a spoon-straw to go with it.

5 juniper berries
2.5 cm/1-inch piece of fresh or candied angelica
1 teaspoon coriander seeds
1 cm/½-inch piece of cinnamon stick
1 teaspoon anise seeds (optional)
1 teaspoon caraway seeds (optional)
170 g/¾ cup sugar
550 ml/2 cups water
9 limes, preferably unwaxed

1. To prepare the sorbet: bash the juniper berries, angelica, coriander, cinnamon stick, and anise and carraway seeds (if using) in a mortar and pestle for a few seconds until bruised.

2. Put the sugar, 170 ml/¾ cup of the water, and the bruised spices into a pan and bring to a simmer, stirring until the sugar dissolves.

3. Wash, pat dry, and zest the limes. As soon as the sugar syrup reaches the simmering point, remove it from the heat, add the lime zest, and place the pan in a sink full of ice water to cool.

4. Juice the limes, then add the juice and the remaining 380 ml/1½ cups water to the spiced syrup. Cover and put into the fridge for at least 3 hours, or until completely chilled.

5. To make the sorbet: strain the mix though a fine-mesh sieve, discarding the zest and spices.

6. Pour the sorbet mix into an ice cream machine and churn according to the machine's instructions until frozen, thick, and snowy-looking, usually 20 to 25 minutes.

7. Scrape the sorbet into a suitable lidded container. Top with a piece of wax paper to limit exposure to air, cover, and freeze for at least 2 hours, or until ready to serve.

Note—I cut lengths of wild angelica in the summer and freeze them to use in this sorbet. You can look for emerald-green candied stems online or in the cake decorating section of specialty shops.

# BARBADOS CUSTARD

This is a light and not-too-sweet ice cream, with a delicious old-fashioned flavor. It's my signature vanilla and is popular all year as it's refreshing in summer yet also excellent served alongside more wintry desserts—I'm thinking of Christmas desserts in particular. This ice cream gets its name from its three defining ingredients: unrefined sugar, vanilla, and rum.

1 vanilla pod
350 ml/1½ cups whole milk
Pinch of sea salt
6 egg yolks
60 g/⅓ cup sugar
60 g/⅓ cup light brown sugar or muscovado sugar
250 ml/1 cup crème fraîche
1 tablespoon dark rum

1. To prepare the ice cream: split the vanilla pod using the tip of a sharp knife, scrape out its seeds, and add both seeds and pod to a non-reactive pan, along with the milk and sea salt. Stir often, using a whisk or silicone spatula, to prevent it from catching. Once the liquid is hot and steaming, whisk the egg yolks and both sugars together in a separate bowl until combined.

2. Pour the hot milk over the yolks in a thin stream, whisking continuously. Return all the mix to the pan and cook over low heat until it reaches 82°C/180°F, stirring all the time to avoid curdling the eggs and keeping a close eye on it so as not to let it boil. As soon as your digital thermometer says 82°C/180°F, place the pan in a sink of ice water.

3. Add the crème fraîche and rum and whisk into the custard. Speed up the cooling process by stirring the mix every so often. Once the custard is at room temperature, scrape it into a clean container, cover with plastic wrap, and chill in the fridge.

4. To make the ice cream: the following day, use a small ladle to push the custard through a fine-mesh sieve or chinois into a clean container. Reserve the vanilla pod (see page 19), then liquidize the cold custard with an immersion blender for a minute.

5. Pour the custard into an ice cream machine and churn according to the machine's instructions until frozen and the texture of stiff whipped cream, 20 to 25 minutes.

6. Scrape the ice cream into a suitable lidded container. Top with a piece of wax paper to limit exposure to air, cover, and freeze until ready to serve.